D1461113

LIFE AFTER DEATH

BLITZ EDITIONS

Published by Blitz Editions
an imprint of Bookmart Ltd
Registered Number 2372865
Trading as Bookmart Ltd, Desford Road, Enderby
Leicester LE9 5AD

Cover design: Peter Dolton
Text design: Jim Reader
Production Manager: Sue Gray
Editorial Manager: Roz Williams

Printed in the Slovak Republic
50975

ISBN 1 85605 130 7

Every effort has been made to contact the copyright holders for the pictures.
In some cases they have been untraceable, for which we offer our apologies.
Thanks to the Fortean Picture Library and the Hulton Deutsch Collection Ltd, who supplied most of them.
Pictures have been provided as follows: M. De Cet (p 68), Estate of Frank Brookesmith (p 7),
Tom Fox (p 67), HarperCollins (p 64 bottom), Hulton Deutsch Collection Ltd (pp 3–6, 8 top, 10 top,
11, 13, 16, 18, 20–6, 28–31, 32 top right and bottom, 33, 34 top, 35, 36, 39–41, 44, 45, 46 top, 47,
50, 51, 53–63, 64 top, 66, 70, 71, 73 left, 74, 77, 78, 79 bottom, 80 bottom),
The Mansell Collection (p 73 right) and Mary Evans Picture Library (pp 75 and 76).
The remainder have been supplied by the Fortean Picture Library.
Cover: The Hulton Deutsch Collection Ltd supplied the pictures at left and top right on the front.
The remainder were supplied by the Fortean Picture Library.

The Author
Reuben Stone has long been fascinated by the paranormal
and the mysteries of the unexplained. He is the author of many books
and articles on military history, popular science and technology,
and various aspects of anomalous phenomena.

LIFE AFTER DEATH

GHOSTS AND APPARITIONS

A troubled lady, haunting the place she was bound to in life; a dead father, unable to rest easy until his will is carried out; a piratical sailor whose love of adventure defeats even death – the many shades of ghosts present intriguing, if inconsistent, evidence for survival beyond the grave.

In 1968, Frances Little and her husband were delighted with the adobe house they had bought in the desert setting of California's Kern County, but after a few weeks, Mr Little became disturbed at seeming to see his wife in two places at once. He'd leave her in one room, or outside, only to see her immediately afterwards, wandering around at the other end of the house. Finally, it dawned on him that the 'other woman' must be a ghost. But whose ghost? And why was she haunting the house?

Then, alone at home one night, Frances Little herself saw a 'tall thin woman in a long dark old-fashioned dress' come out of a back room and go into her bedroom. From there, she went into the family room and Mrs Little was able to see her features quite clearly.

Not long after this, Mrs Little was sorting through some junk that had been left in the garage by the previous owners. To her amazement, she came across a photograph of a woman who looked exactly like the ghost she had seen. Careful enquiries revealed that this was Alice Margaret Kolitisch who, with her husband, had had the adobe house built in the 1920s. She was, Frances Little felt, still concerned about the house she had loved when alive.

This is a ghost story in a classic mould: the troubled shade of the dead haunts a place it had been bound to emotionally in life. But not all ghost stories are like this,

Opposite: *The spectre of the Brown Lady of Raynham Hall, Norfolk, photographed in 1936 as she floats down the stairs of the house. The Brown Lady conforms to the most common notion of a ghost – the shade of a dead person who haunts a place where he or she enjoyed or suffered a crucial emotional experience. But by no means all ghosts fit this pattern.*

The Battle of Gettysburg (below) was a turning point in the American Civil War. During the war's worst days, US President Abraham Lincoln sought help from a medium.

Abraham Lincoln rides in triumph through Richmond, Virginia, on 4 April 1865 (above). Just one week later he was shot dead by the actor John Wilkes Booth (above right) – an event that Lincoln had apparently foreseen in a dream. Lincoln's interest in psychic matters and his mordantly ironic sense of humour may account for his haunting the White House (below right), seen here as it was shortly before Lincoln took up residence as 16th president of the United States.

and because hauntings are so varied in kind, they make intriguing, if inconsistent, evidence for some kind of life after death.

Legend says that US President Abraham Lincoln had a strong belief in ghosts: he apparently consulted a medium during the worst days of the Civil War and, according to W.H. Crook, one of his bodyguards, Lincoln had a number of psychic experiences. At the beginning of April 1865, he told Crook that he had had a dream in which he had been in the hall of the White House, and had seen a coffin draped in black there. When he asked who

it was for, he was told: 'The president.'

On 11 April, Lincoln told Crook that he had dreamed of his own assassination; and on the morning of 14 April he had a vision of a ship carrying him to some unknown place. That night, against the advice of Crook and other members of his staff, Lincoln went to Ford's Theater in Washington. There, he was shot dead by John Wilkes Booth. Within months of Lincoln's death, rumours began to circulate that his ghost was haunting the White House.

Lincoln's spectre took a long time to take

visible form. Theodore Roosevelt, president from 1901 to 1909, maintained that he 'felt the presence' of Lincoln at 1600 Pennsylvania Avenue. The first person actually to see his ghost was Grace Coolidge, wife of Calvin Coolidge, the 30th president, who was in office between 1923 and 1929. Mrs Coolidge saw the ghost standing at the window of the Oval Office, staring out onto Pennsylvania Avenue in the attitude of a man deep in thought. Staff members and presidential aides have reported the same thing – and the apparition always appears at the same window.

The next president, Herbert Hoover (at the White House from 1928 to 1932), heard no more than 'odd sounds' but said that 'many of them were fantastic'.

Between 1932, when Franklin Delano Roosevelt became president, and 1945, when he died, Lincoln's ghost was allegedly seen many times. On one occasion Queen Wilhelmina of the Netherlands, who had long had an interest in spiritualism, had gone to bed in the Lincoln Room – formerly used by Lincoln himself as a dressing room – when she heard a gentle tap on the door. She opened it, and there stood the dead president, gravely doffing his famous

stovepipe hat; then the apparition vanished. When the queen told Roosevelt of her encounter the next morning, he confessed that he knew the room was haunted; Winston Churchill had also seen the ghost of Lincoln while sleeping there, and Mrs Roosevelt had detected Lincoln's presence on several occasions.

Harry S Truman, who succeeded to the presidency on Roosevelt's death and lived in the White House from 1945 to 1952, often joked to his guests about Lincoln's ghost. He once admitted that though he had never seen it, he was certain that he had heard it, in the form of footsteps which approached his bedroom door, followed by a knocking.

There had certainly been no rational explanation for these sounds, he said, and they always occurred in the early hours of the morning. A White House stenographer who served both Roosevelt and Truman allegedly saw Lincoln frequently. The first time was in the Lincoln Room; the spectre was sitting on the bed pulling on his boots. The girl was badly scared, although with repeated appearances she seems to have got used to seeing the ghost. Both John and Robert Kennedy saw the spirit of Lincoln, according to friends of the Kennedy family.

Above: *Franklin D. Roosevelt, 32nd president of the United States. During his tenure at the White House, two distinguished visitors saw the ghost of Lincoln there – Winston Churchill and Queen Wilhelmina of the Netherlands.*

Left: *Grace Goodhue Coolidge, wife of President Calvin Coolidge, who saw Lincoln's ghost in the presidential office on several occasions between 1923 and 1929.*

Right: *Winston Churchill gives his famous 'V for victory' sign. That such a prestigious individual freely admitted to seeing ghosts – Churchill also had a number of remarkably accurate premonitions – argues for the reality of the shade of Lincoln.*

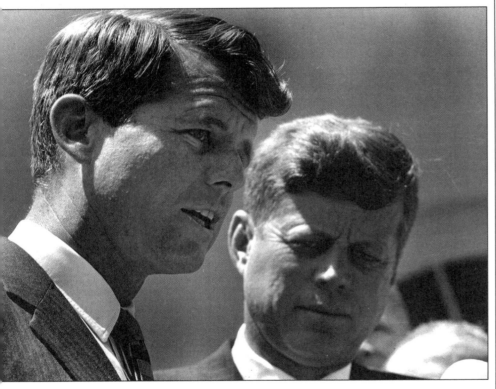

Above: *Robert (left) and John Kennedy. Both brothers saw the Lincoln spectre at the White House during John's presidency, although neither was noted for his interest in psychic or spiritual matters.*

The White House ghost is intriguing for several reasons. First, it hardly seems likely that several presidents, their wives, a queen, and a statesman like Winston Churchill would lie about seeing the wraith of Lincoln: 'seeing ghosts' might call their fitness for high office into question. The credentials of the witnesses, then, are beyond question.

But is this ghost really the spirit of Abraham Lincoln, bound to the scene where he worked and thought so hard and so deeply? Or is the apparition brought into being by something else? Could it be the result of a collective feeling that the White House really ought to be haunted by Lincoln, the greatest of all the men who lived there, and who died so tragically – so that those who have seen him, presidents included, somehow projected the 'spirit' to suit their own unconscious wishes? Or might the apparition be some kind of recording of Lincoln, impressed upon the place somehow and played over and over again? Or is the Lincoln ghost not one ghost, but several – sometimes one thing, sometimes another, depending on the circumstances and the person who perceives it?

Such questions take us to the heart of the mystery surrounding ghosts of all kinds.

HOARSE WHISPERS

What is a ghost? That the belief that a ghost is present and active can be created by circumstances is beyond doubt. Given some specious evidence, a credulous collection of witnesses, and a background of fear, a ghost will make itself heard, seen or felt. This is very clear from the story told by New Zealander Frank Brookesmith, who until his death in 1991 was one of the last few survivors from the age of square-rigged sailing ships.

In his book *I Remember the Tall Ships*, Brookesmith recalled a haunting that briefly afflicted the tanker *Orowaiti* on a voyage across the Pacific from Wellington, New Zealand, to San Francisco, in the early 1920s. What happened was this. After one of the sailors on board the ship had committed suicide, the rest of the crew, understandably distressed at the incident, swore that the dead man was haunting the bow end of the ship. The ghost was invisible, but its constant, eerie whisper could clearly be heard. Determined to find out what was really going on, Brookesmith went forward at about 4 o'clock one morning to investigate.

'The ship was rolling quite moderately and I paced the deck from right forward to the after rail on the weather side. I heard nothing. I walked along the lee side and paused by the windlass.

'I froze, and the hairs on the back of my neck stood on end...It felt as if *all* my hair was standing on end. Someone was talking in a hoarse whisper!…I ran down the ladder to the foredeck and I walked into the space under the focsle head. It was all as dark as the inside of a cow but I knew what was there…I stood quite still and listened. There was no sound save the usual creaks and cracks of a ship in a seaway…

'I went back…to the after rail and I could hear a faint whispering. I could not distinguish the words but there was no mistaking the sound…My skin crept. I knew that I could easily imagine words but I simply had to find the source of the sounds. I moved about and found that, the nearer I was to the gypsy [a small winch], the clearer was the sound. It was an indistinct asthmatic whisper.

'I put my hand on the [anchor] chain where it went down the pipe into [its] locker and I *felt* it! As the ship rolled the rusty links moved against each other to make this harsh sound.

'Rub two pieces of rough iron together and you will hear what we heard,' Brookesmith wrote many years later. 'Add to it unhappiness and superstitious fears and you will have a haunting.' He silenced the 'ghost' by lashing the chain down with rope. 'I've found the ghost and I've bound him hands and feet,' he reported with a certain grim satisfaction.

Frank Brookesmith was, on that occasion at least, driven to get to the root of the shipboard 'haunting' partly by curiosity and partly by a determination not to be prey – or to be in thrall – to what he called 'superstitious fears'. But he also told his family of another and quite different experience of the supernatural that he had as a young man, before he went to sea, in the last years of World War 1.

He was then working as a clerk in a bank in Christchurch, New Zealand; one of the few perks of the job was a free flat above the bank premises. The perk in turn had its price – which was that he had to be on the alert for any attempt to raid the bank. To help terminally dissuade any villains intent on relieving the bank of its customers' cash – or perhaps simply as a psychological support – he was issued with a hefty British Army officer's .455 Webley revolver and several boxes of ammunition. He used most of the ammunition practising with the pistol in the deserted hills outside the town, but he

slept with the weapon loaded at his bedside every night.

One night he awoke suddenly, inexplicably disturbed. Peering warily at first down the length of his bed through half-closed eyes – half-expecting, half-fearing to find an intruder in his room – he found himself staring round-eyed at the figure of a young woman, dressed in white, kneeling as if in prayer beside his bed – and leaning her weightless arms on the covers over his knees.

This apparition, he swore, bore no relation to any image from any dream he had been having immediately prior to waking up. In fact he had been in a dreamless period of sleep when he was so strangely disturbed. What he saw, he admitted, frightened him. But his reaction to this extraordinary sight was weirdly rational: he wondered if it were not some outlandish decoy – the gangsters' moll pretending to be a ghost! – set up by some

Above: *Frank Brookesmith as a seaman in the early 1920s. He experienced two hauntings in these years – one of a spectral young lady, another that seemed to be of a shipmate who had committed suicide. One had an entirely natural explanation, while the other appeared to be a genuine ghost.*

'IT FELT AS IF ALL MY HAIR WAS STANDING ON END. SOMEONE WAS TALKING IN A HOARSE WHISPER!'

Right: *Christchurch, New Zealand, in the 1920s.*

particularly cunning set of burglars. With unusual presence of mind, he reached for his gun. As he swung it into aim, the image of the girl kneeling by his bedside faded away.

Brookesmith found himself rather foolishly waving a heavy revolver at his own bare feet. Making the best of a bad job, he salved his wounded pride by creeping around his flat and then the ground floor – the working area of the bank – looking for any sign of a break-in. He found nothing out of order, but neither could he explain the apparition that had woken him up.

Here we have a witness to two very different kinds of haunting, and a witness, to boot, with a certain rather startlingly logical reaction to both. Unfortunately, we don't know (because he did not say) whether Brookesmith made any attempt to discover if anyone else had ever seen the female phantom that rested so lightly on his bed, or if he made any effort later to find out whose phantom she may have been.

However, the real importance of these two stories, side by side and from the same source, is that someone can on one occasion believe he is really seeing a ghost and accept it as such, and on another occasion, confronted by another apparent haunting, take a thoroughly sceptical view and investigate and effectively exorcize it. To that person – and this is the point – the existence of false ghosts does not preclude the existence of real ones. And no one can say that Brookesmith's extraordinarily cool reaction was essentially different from one case to the other. On each occasion he responded according to a certain logic (despite his fright). The witness, if not the phenomenon, was consistent throughout.

DEATH-OMEN

Does any of this get us any nearer the answer to the question: what is a ghost?

In a way, no, this last story does not, because there is no evidence to suggest that the phantom lady seen by the conscientious bank guard and bluff, no-nonsense sailor Frank Brookesmith was not, in any case, a figment of his own momentarily disoriented imagination. But it does tell us that the most sceptical and practical of people can believe that they have genuinely seen a ghost. In short, the key to ghost stories may be the *witness*, not the ghost. And these two stories together also tell us that the most common presumption about ghosts is that they are the spirits – or at least the inexplicably immaterial records – of people once alive and now dead.

Before sorting out the vexed question of the role of the witness in ghost reports, it's as well to establish how varied the phenomenon of hauntings itself can be.

Ghosts of people may or may not be images of the spirit world, but they are not always apparitions of dead people, or even of animals.

Christina Hole comments in *Haunted England*: 'There is scarcely an old road in England along which the Spectral Coach has not trundled at some time or another. It

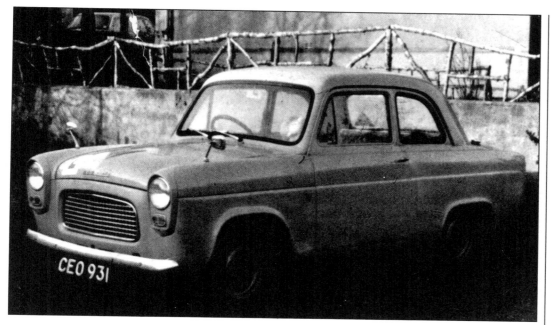

Left: *The head of a phantom small boy mysteriously appeared in this photograph of a 1950s car, taken in March 1974 by David Broadbent of Bradley, Yorkshire.*

THE SPECTRAL COACH WITH ITS BLACK HORSES AND HEADLESS DRIVER IS A DEATH-OMEN FOR THOSE UNLUCKY ENOUGH TO ENCOUNTER IT.

Below: *The spectral coach and coachman, of whom it has been said that 'scarcely an old road in England' lacks an example. But how does a coach acquire a 'spiritual' form, if ghosts are the shades of the dead?*

may be either a genuine coach or a hearse; but whatever form it takes, it bears certain distinguishing marks [that] prove it to be something from another world. It is always black, and so are the driver and his horses. Often both are headless. It appears suddenly on the roadway and moves very fast and usually without noise. Only in a few cases do we hear of the rumble of wheels on the road or the clattering of horses' hoofs to give warning of its approach. Like most apparitions of its kind, it…often serves as a death-omen for those unlucky enough to encounter it.'

Why vehicles should take on spectral form, no one knows (let alone how), but phantom conveyances appear time and

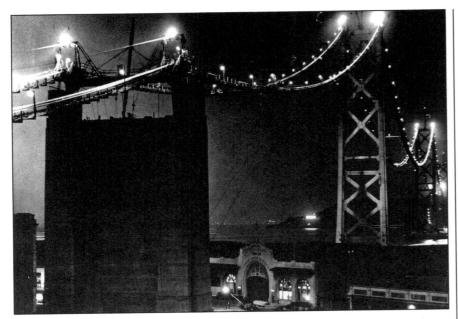

Above: *Golden Gate Bridge, San Francisco Bay, under construction in 1936. Six years later Jack Cornelius and another seaman saw a ghostly sailing ship nearby.*

again in accounts of ghosts and hauntings. Furthermore, this is a tradition that refuses to die (so to speak). Modern accounts of ghost vehicles are rife with phantom trains, buses, ships, cars, and even aircraft.

SPECTRAL SHIP

In the winter of 1942, the destroyer USS *Kennison* was returning from an anti-submarine patrol along the California coast, coming up to the Golden Gate at the mouth of San Francisco Bay, when a heavy fog came out of nowhere. The *Kennison*'s engine-room bells rang for dead slow, and the ship began to nose carefully through the water, its foghorn sounding.

Then the fantail lookout, torpedoman Jack Cornelius, yelled into the ship's tannoy for everyone to look aft. Cornelius and another seaman, who was on the aft gundeck, both reported that a huge, derelict, two-masted sailing ship had passed within a few feet of the destroyer's stern. They had had the hulk in full view for about a half a minute before the fog closed in around it. The radar operators, however, had not seen a thing before, during, or after the sighting of the seemingly immaterial ship.

There is one ghost ship that has been seen dozens of times over the years by sailors. In a letter to *Occult Review* in 1921, F.G. Montagu Powell recounted an incident that had occurred many years previously, when he was serving with the Royal Navy:

'Somewhere in July 1859, when I was on HMS *Euryalus*, we were off the Cape of Good Hope when a curious thing happened. It was about six bells (11 am) in the forenoon, and I was midshipman of the watch, when a dull and heavy mist fell upon us. We were under steam and sail and very light airs from the south were hardly filling our sails, the sun breaking out through the mist like a fiery copper ball every now and then, when we sighted a sailing ship right ahead of us, lying in fact right across our track and so close that before we could hail her or alter our course we were on top of her and in fact cut clean through her.

'Her sails seemed to me flat, lifeless and discoloured, no "bellying to the breeze" about them. Her crew, clad in sou'westers and tarpaulins and the traditional breeches, moved lifelessly about the decks, coiling up ropes or leaning over the hammock netting, and paying not the slightest attention to us, not nearly so much as we paid to them.

'I remember the curious vague look she had as, apparently undamaged by this tremendous impact (though of course there was no impact, it was just like cutting through a shadow or a cloud) she vanished slowly astern, the mist overwhelming and enfolding her like a shroud. I remember hearing one bluejacket saying to another, "Yon's the Flying Dutchman, I expect."'

The Flying Dutchman, Hendrik Vanderdecken, blasphemed against God and was condemned to sail the seas until the Last Judgement. That is a legend. But here we have dates, names, a specific location – and an account of a genuine personal experience. Was this spectral ship the Flying Dutchman? Or did the legend spring up to explain all such ghostly encounters at sea?

RECORDINGS OF THE PAST

In their way, steam trains are no less romantic than full-rigged ships – although no less problematic when it comes to explaining how ghost trains could be in any sense 'spiritual'. But there is no lack of them in the annals of ghost lore.

John Quirk, of Pittsfield, Massachusetts, reported that he and several customers at the Bridge Lunch café saw a phantom train hauled by a steam engine one afternoon in February 1958. The train consisted of a baggage car and five or six coaches, which the witnesses described in great detail. A month later, a similar train passed the same location at top speed, barrelling towards Boston, at 6.30 one morning.

Railroad officials insisted that no steam

engine had run on that line for years. On yet another occasion when the phantom train was reported, the railroad stated categorically that no train of any material kind had been on that section of track at that time.

As trucks have largely replaced trains for hauling freight – and as the trucker and his big rig have become romanticized as modern exemplars of the great American tradition of rugged individualism – so ghost trucks have appeared on the highways.

In *Fate* magazine for February 1986, truck driver Harriette Spanabel of Brooksville, Florida, recalled an experience that unnervingly echoes Steven Spielberg's eerie movie *Duel*:

'I drive a tractor trailer and haul produce from Florida up the East Coast and west as far as Texas. For the past year and a half, always on my return run, a phantom truck follows me at least part of the time. At first I thought it was my imagination. One minute nothing would be behind me but the next minute a tractor trailer would be there.

'This truck has followed me on both Interstate highways and narrow two-lane roads. It is always behind me at night, moving over every once in a while so that its left headlight hits my left mirror directly. It disappears just as quickly as it appears.

'I now know for sure that I am not imagining the truck because I have a witness who also watched my mystery

Above: *US steam locomotive on a special excursion in the 19th century. Many such trains appear in ghostly form – as, increasingly, do trucks.*

Opposite below:
Two phantom faces, photographed from on board the oil tanker SS **Watertown** *in December 1924. The ghost faces apparently had the features of two sailors who had died in an accident on the voyage down the Pacific coast of the USA and had been buried at sea. The faces appeared for days afterwards, though only for brief periods each day.*

THE PHANTOM TRUCK
VANISHES JUST AS QUICKLY
AS IT APPEARS.

Major disasters such as this train crash (opposite) sometimes generate the phenomenon known as a 'near-death apparition'. Victims of the tragedy appear at the point of death to their nearest and dearest – although the witnesses may be hundreds of miles from the fatal event.

vehicle. I recently took my friend Kelly Rose with me to Miami to make a delivery. I picked up the load in Philadelphia on March 8, 1985. It was a load of dry freight with two drops. It was when we were coming back from Miami that the truck first joined us at approximately 11:30 the evening of the 12th. I drove out of Lakeland, Fla, on US 98 going north. I planned to turn onto [State Route] 471 which runs through the middle of the Green Swamp. The phantom truck first appeared behind us on US 98 about two miles before I made my turn onto [State Route] 471. It followed us from there until we had almost reached [State Route] 50 where I turn to go west into the town where I live.

'On a narrow two-lane road which runs through a state forest, about 50 miles from my house, the truck again appeared behind us. Kelly immediately asked where it had come from. Of course I couldn't tell her but it followed us for 30 miles before it disappeared this time.

'Kelly, who had been watching the truck intently in her mirror, was astounded. I stopped my truck on 471 and we got out and looked for the other truck. It was completely gone. On this road there are no side roads where a truck could pull on or off. There are no shoulders where a truck could pull off without either tipping over or ending up tangled in a mass of big trees. And let me add there was no other traffic on 471 going in either direction.'

There is no difficulty in believing that these various witnesses are telling the truth – especially as in each case there was more than one witness to the strange events they describe. But these phantoms of the inanimate can hardly be spirits of something dead – since they weren't alive in the first place. So we may be forced to conclude that many ghosts are some kind of recording of the past. But then the problem still remains as to why a particular train, ship or even mighty, snarling 18-wheel semi-trailer should record itself on a particular place: why them, and not any of the hundreds of others that have passed that way?

GHOULISH APPEARANCE

Probably the most frequently told of all kinds of ghost story are those concerning apparitions of people at the moment of their death. Here at least the ghost is inextricably linked with the notion of a life after death – or, at least, with some kind of spiritual existence that is able to project itself across time and space from the dying person to someone near or dear to them. Two instances of this kind of haunting – if that is the word – show how different they can be.

One morning in the spring of 1973, 58-year-old Mrs Martha Beckwhite was doing one of the things she likes best – working in her garden – in Blandford, Dorset. Without warning she felt, without knowing how she could identify it, the presence of one of her youngest daughter's friends, Luke Fore. Then, she distinctly heard his voice say 'Goodbye, Martha'. Again without knowing why, she knew that he had died. When the telephone rang in the evening of that day and she heard her daughter's voice on the line, she said: 'Don't worry, darling; I know why you've called. Luke's just died, hasn't he?'

Indeed he had, of cancer of the liver. Two things about this case are intriguing, however. First was that she had met Luke Fore only once or twice (he was the husband of one of her daughter's closest friends at the time). Second was that she had no idea that Luke was ill. For various reasons Luke's cancer had been kept a secret from everyone but his immediate family: no one outside that small circle knew that he even had a cold, let alone was terminally ill.

There are two ways of stating the mystery here. Whatever the ultimate answer, there may be some clue in the fact that Martha Beckwhite and Luke Fore got along famously together on the few occasions that they met, although they were perhaps 20 years apart in age. Why did he appear to her, though, whom he had met but a few times? Or perhaps the problem should be put another way: why and how did she alone of all the people who knew Luke (and many knew him more intimately) 'tune in' to the fact of his death? Whatever the answer, there is no doubt that Martha Beckwhite received and understood, by some paranormal means, a message from someone who was dying, and whom she had no reason to suppose was even remotely at risk of death.

A much more typical case of a near-death apparition was recounted in the

October 1957 edition of *Fate* magazine.

Mary Travers was sitting up late waiting for her husband George, who was an insurance salesman, to come home. Shortly after the clock struck 11, she heard a cab coming down the street. It stopped in front of the house, and Mrs Travers heard a voice, presumably the driver's, call out 'Good night!' Then she recognized the familiar sound of her husband's steps on the porch. She hurried to the front door to welcome him home.

He came in silently, with his hat pulled down over his eyes, and then he stood with his back to his wife while she shut the door. She thought he was behaving oddly, and asked did he feel all right? He turned to face her – and in place of George's face she saw a hideous white death-mask. She screamed, and continued to scream, so that the neighbours rushed in to see what was wrong. By then, the apparition had vanished. Minutes later the phone rang: the caller regretfully announced that George Travers had been killed in a train crash.

It is difficult to account for such an apparition except as a spirit of the dead. It seems unlikely that by sheer coincidence Mrs Travers imagined his ghoulish appearance on the very night he died. It makes more sense to assume that the spectre was indeed her husband's spirit, or at least a projection from his mind, sent to warn Mrs Travers – albeit silently and shockingly – of what had happened to him.

AS SHE HURRIED TO WELCOME HER HUSBAND HOME SHE SAW THAT WHERE HIS FACE SHOULD HAVE BEEN THERE WAS A HIDEOUS WHITE DEATH-MASK.

THE DEAD MAN'S WILL

The classic example of a haunting that seems to prove the continued existence of an individual in some form after death is the famous case of the 'lost' will of the North Carolina farmer James L. Chaffin. This is one of the best-documented cases in all psychic research. As several writers have remarked, even the lawyers involved seem to have been honest.

James L. Chaffin, a farmer of Davie County, North Carolina, had four sons: John, James, Marshall and Abner. On 16 November 1905 he made a will, attested by two witnesses, leaving everything he owned to his third son, Marshall. Why he singled out Marshall, no one knows. But, a little over 13 years later, the old man had a change of heart. He made a new will. It read:

'After reading the 27th chapter of Genesis I, James L. Chaffin, do make my last will and testament and here it is. I want, after giving my body a decent burial, my little property to be equally divided between my four children…and if she is living, you must take care of your mammy. Witness my seal and hand. James L. Chaffin. This January 16, 1919.'

This second will lacked the signatures of any witnesses, but would be legally valid under the laws of North Carolina if it could be established that the whole of the document was in the testator's own handwriting. Chaffin, unknown to anyone at the time, put the will between two pages of the family Bible on which were printed the 27th chapter of Genesis. The paper was folded over to make a kind of pocket. Chaffin never mentioned the second will to anyone, but he did scribble on a roll of paper, which he stitched into an inside pocket of his overcoat, a note that said: 'Read the 27th chapter of Genesis in my daddie's old Bible.'

On 7 September 1921, James L. Chaffin died unexpectedly after a fall. Marshall, the third son, obtained probate without fuss; there was no reason for anyone to challenge the will, and there was no enmity or rivalry among Chaffin's children.

But in June 1925 the second son, James P. Chaffin, began having vivid dreams that his father was standing silently beside his bed. A week or so later the apparition, dressed in the old black overcoat his son knew so well, spoke: 'You will find my will in my overcoat pocket.' James was convinced this was significant, and hurried to his mother's house.

His father's coat, however, had been given to her eldest son, John, who lived some 20 miles away. James went to John's home, and explained the situation. The two brothers examined the coat together. They found that the inside pocket had been stitched closed; when they cut it open, they found inside the rolled-up strip of paper in their father's handwriting. 'Read the 27th chapter of Genesis in my daddie's old Bible' was not a will, as James's dream had indicated, but the two brothers felt they must follow the message up.

John felt he could not look at the family Bible without independent witnesses, and took a neighbour, the neighbour's daughter, and his own wife and daughter with him. After a long search in his mother's house the old Bible was discovered in a top drawer in an upstairs room and, as it was

Below: *No natural explanation has been found for the ghostly image in this picture. But in 1991, 2-year-old Greg Maxwell* (seated) *began to point upwards and say, 'Old Nanna's here', although no one was visible to anyone but the child. Is this the shade of his dead grandmother?*

being taken out, it fell into three pieces. The neighbour picked up the front section containing Genesis, and it opened automatically at the place indicated in the cryptic message. There lay the second will.

This will was tendered for probate in 1925. Marshall Chaffin had died a year after his father, but his widow contested the application on behalf of her young son.

The court assembled in December 1925 to decide the issue: the public areas were crowded at the prospect of seeing a classic family squabble burst into open view. The scandal-hungry locals were to be disappointed. On the advice of her lawyer, Marshall's widow withdrew her opposition when she saw the will itself, unmistakably in the old man's handwriting.

There are really only two stark alternatives in explaining this case. Either the Chaffin brothers were lying, and set up the whole elaborate hoax in order to lay their hands on their share of their father's estate, or the story is true from start to finish. But the business of the Chaffin will is one of the best-documented and best-attested cases in ghost lore; and as such it stands as reasonable proof that in some cases, at least, ghosts do represent the consciousness of the dead – and that the physically dead do survive in some form of afterlife.

LOVE OF ADVENTURE

Some famous hauntings, however, leave one wondering to what extent some ghosts are purely subjective entities, existing solely in the mind of the witness.

Captain Joshua Slocum, the great American sailor, had a remarkable experience in July 1895, while on his historic solo voyage around the world in his sloop *Spray*. In the Atlantic, between the Azores and Gibraltar, he ran into squally weather. At the same time he began to suffer an attack of severe stomach cramps. These so distracted him that he went below – without taking in sail as he should have done. He threw himself on the floor of the boat's cabin, in great pain. In his account of the voyage he described what happened next:

'How long I lay there I could not tell, for I became delirious. When I came to, as I thought, from my swoon, I realized that the sloop was plunging into a heavy sea, and looking out of the companionway, to my amazement I saw a tall man at the helm. His rigid hand, grasping the spokes of the wheel, held them as in a vice. One may imagine my astonishment. His rig was that of a foreign sailor, and the large red cap he wore was cockbilled over his left ear, and all was set off with shaggy black whiskers.

'I GAZED UPON HIS THREATENING ASPECT AND WONDERED IF HE HAD COME TO CUT MY THROAT.'

Right: *Christopher Columbus, whose first expedition to the Americas in 1492 consisted of three ships, among them the* **Pinta,** *a caravel. Over 300 years later, Captain Joshua Slocum believed he was visited by the ghost of the pilot of the* **Pinta** *while sailing in the Atlantic. The spectral sailor guided the ship safely through a ferocious storm while Slocum lay in a delirium.*

Right: *Henry, Lord Brougham, who made a pact with a college friend that whichever of the pair died first would appear as a ghost to the other. Brougham's friend kept his word, and showed a mischievous sense of humour in doing so.*

He would have been taken for a pirate in any part of the world. While I gazed upon his threatening aspect I forgot the storm, and wondered if he had come to cut my throat. This he seemed to divine.

'"Senor," said he, doffing his cap, "I have come to do you no harm." And a smile, the faintest in the world, but still a smile, played on his face, which seemed not unkind when he spoke. "I am one of Columbus' crew, the pilot of the *Pinta*, come to aid you. Lie quiet, senor captain, and I will guide your ship tonight. You have a *calentura* [a reference to the stomach cramps] but you will be all right tomorrow…You did wrong to mix cheese with plums…"

'I thought what a very devil he was to carry sail. Again, as if he read my mind, he exclaimed, "Yonder is the *Pinta* ahead, we must overtake her. Give her sail, give her sail!"'

Next day Slocum found that the *Spray* was still on the same heading as he had left her when he staggered below in his 'swoon'.

'Columbus himself could not have held her more exactly on her course,' he wrote. 'I felt grateful to the old pilot, but I marvelled some that he had not taken in the jib. I was getting much better now, but was very weak…I fell asleep. Then who should visit me but my old friend of the night before, this time, of course, in a dream. "You did well last night to take my

advice," said he, "and if you would, I should like to be with you often on the voyage, for the love of adventure alone." He again doffed his cap, and disappeared as mysteriously as he came. I awoke with the feeling that I had been in the presence of a friend and a seaman of vast experience.'

Perhaps so. And perhaps, in his delirious state, Slocum imagined, or hallucinated, the whole thing. But if he did, another small miracle seems to have occurred: the *Spray* kept her course, with no one at the wheel, through a long bout of foul weather and a hostile sea.

'MERE' COINCIDENCE?

The best evidence that some ghosts present proof of a life after death comes from pacts made between friends or relatives in which each party promises that whichever dies first will 'come back' to the other to show that they still survive.

The best-known of these cases is that of Henry, Lord Brougham (1778–1868), the famous and fiery British reformer. Brougham made just such a pact with his old college friend Geoffrey Garner, one that eventually unravelled in a manner so hilarious that it has to be true. Some years after making this agreement, Brougham went travelling in Sweden with a group of friends.

'Arriving at a decent inn, we decided to stop for the night,' he recalled. 'I was glad to take advantage of a hot bath before I turned in, and here a most remarkable thing happened to me – so remarkable that I must tell the story from the beginning.

'After I left the [Edinburgh] High School, I went with Garner, my most intimate friend, to attend the classes in the University...We frequently discussed and speculated upon many grave subjects – among others, on the immortality of the soul, and on a future state. This question, and the possibility, I will not say of ghosts walking, but of the dead appearing to the living, were subjects of much speculation: and we actually committed the folly of drawing up an agreement, written in our blood, to the effect that whichever of us died the first should appear to the other, and thus solve any doubts we had entertained of the "life after death".

'After we had finished our classes at the college, Garner went to India, having got an appointment there in the Civil Service. He seldom wrote to me, and after a lapse of a few years I had almost forgotten him; moreover, his family having little connection with Edinburgh, I seldom saw or heard anything, and I had nearly forgotten his existence.

'I had taken a warm bath, and while lying in it and enjoying the comfort of the heat, after the late freezing I had undergone, I turned my head round, looking toward the chair on which I had deposited my clothes, as I was about to get out of the bath. On the chair sat Garner, looking calmly at me.

'How I got out of the bath I know not, but on recovering my senses I found myself sprawling on the floor. The apparition, or whatever it was, that had taken the likeness of Garner, had disappeared.'

On his return to Edinburgh after this farcical episode, Brougham learned that Garner had died in India on 19 December, the precise date of the apparition. Many years after the event, Brougham tended to be sceptical about it:

'Singular coincidence! yet when one reflects on the vast numbers of dreams which night after night pass through our brains, the number of coincidences between the vision and the event are perhaps fewer and less remarkable than a fair calculation of chances would warrant us to expect. I believe every such seeming miracle is, like every ghost story, capable of explanation.'

Others, too, have suggested these cases are the result of 'mere' coincidence. But in their monumental collection *Phantasms of the Living*, published in 1886, the Society for Psychical Research described nine examples of an apparition following on a pact of this kind. It is surely stretching scepticism to breaking point to suggest that *all* these apparitions are purely 'coincidental' with the death of the parties concerned, especially when such a pact is involved. And even if they are, the sceptics still cannot satisfactorily explain *what* those phantasms are or where they come from.

Nevertheless, it is clear from the apparitions and spectres we have discussed in this chapter that ghost stories, however well documented and however fascinating they may be, do not make the best or most consistent evidence for life after death. That evidence comes in subtler and, often, even stranger forms.

Above: *Borley Rectory, dubbed 'the most haunted house in England', showing the gates at which a ghostly nun was allegedly seen. The dubious nature of the investigations of the phenomena at Borley has led many to wonder since if the house was haunted at all – but the legend lingers on.*

ANOTHER TIME, ANOTHER LIFE

The ancient Celts were terrible in battle as they had no fear of death – they would even lend money on the understanding that if it were not repaid in this life, it would be in the next. What made them so sure that this was not the only life?

The idea that the soul may journey through time, using successive human bodies as vehicles for the journey and the lives of those personalities it adopts as food for its spiritual journey to perfection, is foreign to Western thought. Judaism, Christianity and Islam differ widely in their notions of the kind of afterlife that awaits us, and of heaven and hell, but their broad message is the same.

'It is appointed for men to die once,' says St Paul in his epistle to the Hebrews, 'and after that comes judgement.' If we live in an upright, tolerant and kindly fashion, we shall be rewarded in the life to come – and if we do not, we shall be punished. The fundamental belief is that this is the only life each of us has, and that this life is the only chance we have to prove ourselves morally and spiritually.

So deep is this idea ingrained in Western thought that even in the increasingly irreligious 20th century it has actually proved possible to make money by gently mocking any idea of reincarnation at all. The New York journalist Don Marquis made a small fortune from regaling an eager public with the adventures of his characters Archie, the cockroach who had formerly been a *vers libre* poet but continued to write his versified diary by jumping up and down on the keys of a typewriter, and Mehitabel, the alley cat

who 'once accused herself of being Cleopatra'.

However, belief in reincarnation is widespread, ancient and powerful, and the religions of some of the world's greatest civilizations have held that reincarnation may be combined with transmigration – the entry of the soul into the body of an animal. Such beliefs were common in the West before the rise of Christianity. One reason why the ancient Celts were so devastating as warriors was that they had absolutely no fear of death – so convinced were they of the reality of reincarnation and the continuity of their consciousness. They would even lend money on the understanding that if it could not be repaid in this life, it surely would in a future one.

The torments of Hell (above, as envisaged in a 12th-century illustration) *are one possible outcome of a single earthly lifetime granted the human soul, according to the great Western religions. Others, such as Buddhism, however, believe that the soul may journey towards its fate through many earthly lives. Whenever the Dalai Lama* (opposite) *dies, Tibetan Buddhists make a special search for the child in whom they believe the soul of their leader has been reincarnated.*

Above: *A wealthy household in ancient Athens. The Greeks, for all their famous rationalism and philosophy, believed both in a pantheon of gods notorious for uproarious behaviour, and in personal reincarnation.*

PYTHAGORAS CLAIMED TO REMEMBER HIS PREVIOUS LIVES AS A FISHERMAN, PEASANT, SHOPKEEPER'S WIFE — AND PROSTITUTE.

DEATH AND BIRTH

In ancient Greece, belief in reincarnation was not incompatible with belief in the orthodox pantheon of gods. The Orphic sect, which flourished about 100 years before the golden age of Athens, had a view of earthly life that for gloom and self-punishment matched that of the most zealous medieval Christian flagellator. The Orphics called human existence a 'sorrowful weary wheel', and the only way to escape it was to live with the utmost self-denial and asceticism. Even then, only after many physical deaths and rebirths in both animal and human form would the soul be free.

The belief in reincarnation as such in ancient Greece was not confined to such killjoy cults, however. The mathematical genius Pythagoras, who lived around 500 BC, claimed to know that in former lives he had been variously a fisherman, a peasant, a shopkeeper's wife and a (female) prostitute. Pythagoras, it is true, also held fast to many quite eccentric beliefs, including some concerning the certain fearsome consequences of eating beans.

But Plato, one of the most profoundly original minds of the ancient world, was convinced of the truth of reincarnation. He held that the soul chose its new life at the moment of death, and might enter one of nine levels of being. Plato believed that this was not an endless cycle, and the soul was neither eternal nor did it necessarily progress, or even learn, spiritually from one life to another. Progress could be made if a soul chose its next life wisely, but Plato held that in creating a new physical body for its next life, the soul expended energy. Once its energy was finally consumed, the soul itself died out.

The Roman notion of reincarnation was somewhat different; the 1st-century AD political thinker Sallust, for example, maintained that children born with handicaps were bearing punishments for evils they had committed in former lives.

The other great ancient culture that firmly believed in reincarnation was Egypt. At first, the Egyptian religions held that only 'great souls', destined to lead mankind, were born again, but this belief gradually relaxed and expanded to include everyone from the highest to the lowest social classes. By the time the *Book of the Dead* came to be compiled, matters had become distinctly formalized. The book contains incantations that would free the

Left: *The Sphinx, with the Great Pyramid in the background. These monuments were part of the ancient Egyptians' massive and elaborate system of belief and ritual concerning the afterlife. The Egyptians believed in transmigration as well as reincarnation – the soul might return to earthly life as a plant or an animal or in human form.*

Below: *The prophet Muhammad besieges a castle in the course of spreading his new religious vision. Islam replaced many local animistic religions in the Middle East, and gradually suppressed older beliefs in reincarnation.*

soul from its earthly prison in the tomb and prepare it for reincarnation. And it might come back as a plant – a lotus, say, or a sycamore – or as an animal; after 3000 years of such transmigrations it would be ready to be reborn as a human being once again.

RETURN OF THE GODS

Christianity gradually expunged such ideas as it spread west from the Middle East, and seven centuries later Islam suppressed them as it began to spread south and east. But in places where these religions have arrived only within the last few centuries, native faiths continue to hold fast in their belief in reincarnation.

Throughout the Pacific, for instance, reincarnation is a bulwark of most native religions. The religions of many American Indian tribes endorse reincarnation, too. It has even been suggested that one reason why the 16th-century Spanish *conquistadores* found it so easy to conquer huge tracts of South and Central America, despite the existence of highly developed civilizations there, was the prevailing local belief in reincarnation. The Spanish leaders were seen as reborn, returning gods: in Mexico as Quetzalcoatl, and in Peru as Virochas. The Spanish lost no time in taking advantage of this 'heathen' error, and laid the country waste.

In Alaska, where gold and oil rushes have had more effect on local culture than any missionaries, the indigenous Tlingit people have retained to this day a powerful reverence for reincarnation, which they

> **THE AZTECS BELIEVED THEIR GODS HAD BEEN REBORN — AND THIS BELIEF LED TO THEIR DOWNFALL.**

regard as a direct and immediate continuity from one life to another. Tlingit women pay careful heed to their dreams when they are pregnant, for it is then, in dreams, that a previously incarnated but now disembodied soul announces its intention to them to be reborn in the body of the new baby. At birth, diviners take great care to ascertain whose soul has been reborn, and then the baby is given the tribal name of the person it had been before. The child then takes credit for the good deeds done by its predecessors – but also has a powerful moral example that it must live up to.

THE WHEEL OF REBIRTH

In India, attachment to the idea of reincarnation has never wavered since the Hindu religion took hold and, some 3000 years ago, its sacred writings began to reflect a belief in rebirth and reincarnation. In the *Bhagavad-Gita* ('The Song of Krishna'), the warrior, hero and god Krishna explains that he is the eighth incarnation of the god Vishnu, saying to Arjuna: 'Both I and thou have passed through many births. Mine are known to me, but thou knowest not of thine.' Hindus call reincarnation *samsara*, 'the wheel of rebirth'.

For Hindus, the number of reincarnations one may go through is infinite (and may include transmigration to lower forms of life, or even into rocks and stones), for the purpose of them is to give the soul the opportunity to rid itself of the imperfections that inevitably afflict it from its creation. Between each incarnation the soul enjoys a period of rest, in which it ponders on its progress towards *moksha*, the Absolute, which is also perfection and liberation – from which, paradoxically, the soul first emerged.

To rid oneself of these congenital flaws requires turning one's back on the world and realizing one's best, true nature. At the same time *karma*, the law of cause and effect, is at work: in essence this means that good is rewarded and evil is punished, and what is good or evil for the soul is judged on deeds and effects, not (as in Western religions) on intentions. Thus the *Upanishads* say quite clearly, 'Those whose conduct has been evil will have an evil birth as a dog, a pig, or an untouchable outcast.'

Earthly life is regarded as a burden, and at the same time as an illusion, called *maya*. The opportunities that this ostensibly unworldly outlook, combined with the rigid Hindu caste system, have offered for the exploitation of the poor by the rich have been plentiful, and usually avidly grasped.

THE SEARCH FOR THE DALAI LAMA

This observable corruption of a high ideal may have contributed to the inspiration of Siddartha Gautama, born a Brahman, the highest Hindu caste, around 566 BC. He was the heir to the crown of the Sakya clan on the Ganges in India, and is now known universally as Buddha.

The legend says that as soon as he was born Buddha vowed to end birth, old age, suffering, and death – in short, to break the endless grip of earthly life upon the soul. By the age of 29 he had realized that all were inescapable, and eventually propounded his Four Truths: that existence is suffering, and suffering is inevitable; that suffering is caused by desire; that eliminating desire will rid one of suffering; and that the right conduct – the Eightfold Path – will rid one of desire.

Central to these principles was the belief that the soul was not (as Hinduism taught) an individual and personal thing, which

Below: *A Hindu raja celebrates the festival of Krishna with his wives. In orthodox Hindu belief, social class – caste – was related to the degree of virtue the soul had shown in a previous incarnation.*

Left: *The present Dalai Lama, born in 1935. About three years later, he was recognized as the reincarnation of his predecessor.*

Below: *A 12th-century gilt lacquer Chinese figure of Buddha. Born around 566 BC in India as Siddartha Gautama, Buddha radically questioned the Hindu attitude to reincarnation with which he had grown up, and so became the founder of a new religion.*

drove the cycle of reincarnation. Rather, reincarnation was fuelled by the ego, which was constantly changing from life to life, and was an illusion besides. Rid oneself of ego, therefore, and one would attain *nirvana* – which does not mean heaven or the absolute, but simply extinction. Buddhism thus rejects any connection between social caste and the condition of the soul, although successive rebirths are inevitable if one is to work off the burden of *karma* from previous existences. But this is a matter of purifying the life force, not redeeming the individual.

One of the most fascinating ways in which the Buddhist belief in rebirth has

Dequevauviller sc.

Above: *Constantine, emperor of Rome early in the 4th century* AD. *According to testimony given under hypnosis by Welsh housewife Jane Evans, she had once lived as the wife of Constantine's tutor during his residence in Britain.*

THE SIGNS WERE PLAIN TO THOSE WHO COULD READ THEM: THE CORPSE, THE STAR-SHAPED FUNGUS, AND THE DRAGON FLOWER.

---

practical effect is in the search for a successor to the Dalai Lama, leader of Tibet's Buddhists, when he dies.

The Dalai Lama is regarded as the incarnation of Chenrezi, the Buddhist god of grace, and he has taken earthly form 14 times since 1391. Each time the Dalai Lama (the term means 'greatest teacher') dies, the lamas of Tibet have the task of finding his reincarnated form – a male child born after the death – who will then be brought up to take on the leadership of the Tibetan Buddhist community. When the 13th Dalai Lama died in 1933, it took the monks six years to find his successor.

The search involves sifting a variety of normal and paranormal clues: the lamas scrutinize astrological signs, visions, dreams, and other omens to establish where they should start their quest. After the 13th Dalai Lama's death, the corpse itself offered one clue. It turned its head toward the north-east. Then, in the mausoleum where he was laid, a star-shaped fungus grew on the north-east wall. In the main

courtyard of the monastery housing the tomb, a dragon flower unexpectedly grew by the north-east wall.

The lamas decided that it was in this direction that they should begin their search. To help them came a vision in a dream granted to one of the monastery's monks. He saw a place sacred to Buddhists – the lake at Chos Khorgyal, in China, and also a house with carved gables and eaves painted blue. Near here, the lamas concluded, they would find the child they were seeking.

In 1937 a group of lamas and monks set off for China to find the house. Two years later, at the village of Takster, they found it. One of the high lamas in the party disguised himself as a servant and went into the house. He found inside a two-year-old boy, Tenzin Gyatso, who instantly demanded the rosary that, beneath his disguise, the lama was wearing around his neck. This was not the lama's – but it had belonged to the Dalai Lama. Tenzin Gyatso then identified – or recognized – other rosaries, a drum and a walking-stick that had also belonged to the former Dalai Lama.

Encouraged by these initial signs, the lamas went on to look for physical confirmation that the boy was the current embodiment of Chenrezi. The various bodily characteristics, moles and birth-marks found on every Dalai Lama were indeed in place, and the lamas set about making arrangements for the boy and his family to travel to Tibet. Among these was paying a $300,000 ransom to the provincial governor for allowing Tenzin Gyatso to leave China, but eventually the infant Dalai Lama was installed in the Potala Palace above Lhasa to begin his long and arduous training to become the spiritual and temporal leader of the Tibetan nation.

The alleged reincarnation of the Tibetan Dalai Lama is not, in itself, proof of the reality of repeated rebirth. Without casting doubt on the sincerity of those involved, one could if one wanted pick holes in a number of aspects even in this one case. And the key to the matter, here, is profound religious belief; driven by that, a sceptic would assert, the law of averages says that sooner or later the lamas are bound to find a suitable child to proclaim as their reincarnated leader.

On the other hand, there are many cases from the West, where there is no established traditional belief in reincarnation or rebirth, of people who to their own surprise have discovered that they have apparently lived more than one life on Earth.

THE SECRET MEMORY

The evidence for these claims has been gathered exclusively from hypnotic regression – that is, from subjects who have been hypnotized and then led back into the past to recall what they can of any former lives. Unfortunately, the most plausible of these – notably the alleged reincarnation of the Irish woman Bridey Murphy (1798–1864, according to the account given under hypnosis) as Wisconsin housewife Virginia Tighe (born in 1923), and the various lives recounted by Welsh housewife Jane Evans – have fallen apart in the light of detailed research.

Of these, the claims of Jane Evans were the most transparent. Once researcher Melvin Harris had burrowed into them, they looked more like a highly aerated Swiss cheese than evidence for reincarnation.

Jane Evans produced an astonishing wealth of detail about (for instance) life as the wife of the tutor to the young Constantine (later to be Emperor of Rome) in 4th-century Britain, or as a young Jewess caught up in the massacre of the Jews in York in 1190. This latter account in fact contained a wealth of thoroughly *inaccurate* information both about York and about the Jews of the 12th century, and most of it seems to have come from a play broadcast on BBC radio.

Jane Evans's life as 'Livonia' in 4th-century Roman Britain was taken almost word for word from a novel called *The Living Wood* by Louis de Wohl. It seems that Jane Evans had, quite honestly, forgotten that she had ever read any of the books on which her 'former lives' were based, but retrieved her memories of them from her subconscious while in a hypnotic trance. This phenomenon, known as cryptomnesia (from the Greek for 'secret memory') is familiar to hypnotherapists, and has indeed proved useful in digging out facts – often traumatic – about their subjects' early lives that they have often deliberately forgotten.

Another detailed recall of an actual historical event was provided by a subject known only as 'Jan' when she was put into trance by hypnotist Joe Keeton. Jan became 18-year-old Joan Waterhouse who, she said, was tried for witchcraft at Chelmsford Assizes, Essex, in 1556. All the details were proven to be historically correct – including the existence of Joan Waterhouse and her presence in the dock. The only original source for Jan's – or Joan's – account that survived in the 20th century was a contemporary pamphlet, and the only surviving copy was in the library of the Archbishop of Canterbury's London residence, Lambeth Palace. Jan swore that she had never been there and had never seen the document.

> **THE WOMAN BECAME AN 18-YEAR-OLD GIRL WHO HAD BEEN TRIED FOR WITCHCRAFT OVER 400 YEARS AGO.**

But there was one bizarre anomaly. As Joan, Jan insisted that she had been tried in the reign of Queen Elizabeth I. Unfortunately, the English monarch in 1556 was Queen Mary I; Elizabeth did not accede to the throne until 1558. Given the ferment in religious life at the time, the supreme importance of the monarch in deciding and directing what religious practices were acceptable, and the sensitivity to such matters of people at the local level and their readiness to act in their own obsessive interests, this seems an extraordinary confusion.

And, indeed, there was an extraordinary

Above: *Lambeth Palace, London residence of the archbishops of Canterbury. Here was the only known copy of an account of a 16th-century witch trial held in Cheltenham, Essex. Its details were reproduced with uncanny – but crucially flawed – accuracy by a subject of hypnotic regression who claimed to be the reincarnation of one of the accused.*

THE CAUTIOUS PROFESSOR BELIEVED THE CASES WERE 'SUGGESTIVE OF REINCARNATION'.

confusion – in the mind of Joe Keeton and his subject 'Jan' – about what constitutes proper research. For the Lambeth Palace pamphlet had been reprinted during the 19th century, its solid black-letter type substituted by a fair attempt to reproduce a more legible typeface and design of Shakespeare's time. But there was one crucial error. The 19th-century printer had set the date of the Chelmsford witchcraft trial as 1556 – the date insisted upon by Jan and Joan. But the original plainly reads 1566 – by which time Queen Elizabeth had been on the throne for eight somewhat tempestuous years.

The only logical conclusion is that Jan had not, as she and Joe Keeton thought, once existed as Joan Waterhouse, accused of witchcraft, but had read, absorbed and – to be charitable – forgotten the reprint of the 16th-century trials at Chelmsford. But Keeton did not do this fundamental piece of research: a sceptic had to do it, and so debunk the case.

Perhaps the final word on hypnosis and progressive reincarnation should go to a travel courier who, in the late 1980s, was accompanying a group of middle-aged American ladies on the Nile steamer from Port Said to Luxor. In the middle of a conversation about the politics of the Middle East, she said to this author: 'You think you got problems? I've got *nine Cleopatras* on this tour with me. You try keeping *them* from fighting.'

Right: *An engraving from Zucchero's portrait of Queen Elizabeth I of England. The date of her accession to the throne, 1558, was the key to revealing the alleged reincarnation of the Cheltenham witch Joan Waterhouse.*

A MATTER OF FAITH

Is there, then, any real evidence for reincarnation?

Actually, and sadly for those of us who would like to have another crack at life in the hope that we might not make the same terrible mistakes again, the answer is most likely a resounding 'No'.

Some of the most apparently convincing evidence for reincarnation has come from the researches of Dr Ian Stevenson, professor of psychology at the University of Virginia. Dr Stevenson has travelled the world, conducted innumerable in-depth interviews, and assiduously researched and reported a huge collection of cases that are, in his cautious words, 'suggestive of reincarnation'.

The British historian Ian Wilson has noted a number of problematic inconsistencies in Stevenson's evidence, and has also pointed out two particular but telling consistencies.

First, Stevenson has had to rely, on his extensive travels, on interpreters who generally already shared a belief in reincarnation with those he was interviewing. In some cultures people will tend to tell foreign visitors what they *think* the stranger wants to hear rather than the precise truth as they know it.

Second, Wilson has completed a careful analysis of the social backgrounds of the children claiming to have been reincarnated and compared them with the families of the people they allegedly once were. In an astonishing preponderance of cases, the family that the 'reincarnated' child has claimed to belong to has been of higher social status – from anything to an artisan (as opposed to a peasant) to a millionaire (as opposed to – a peasant). In a society in which belief in reincarnation is basic, and that is also circumscribed by a class system that is deeply underwritten by religious orthodoxy, any evidence that offers escape from certain wretched individual circumstances will surely be grasped at the earliest opportunity. Wilson does not say so directly, but it is not difficult to suspect from his evidence that the families involved in the claims Dr Stevenson has investigated have perhaps coached the children in question.

The truth or otherwise of reincarnation, then, has to remain, for the time being at least, a matter of faith. This does not mean that reincarnation does not occur – perhaps only for some people and not for others – but it does mean that there is no conclusive evidence for it at the moment.

It is still an attractive idea. And it remains a bulwark of many ancient and respected cultures around the world.

¶ The Apprehenſion and confeſsion of three notorious Witches. Arreigned and by Iuſtice condemned and executed at *Chelmeſ-forde*, in the Countye of Eſſex, *the 5. day of Iulye, laſt paſt.* 1589.
¶ With the manner of their diueliſh practices and keeping of their ſpirits, whoſe fourmes are heerein truelye proportioned.

IOAN PRENTIS & hir Bid

TACK

GILL

Above: *Account of the execution of three witches at Chelmsford, Essex, in 1589. Under hypnosis, Joan Waterhouse appeared to recall being tried there for witchcraft some years earlier – but there was a significant anomaly regarding the date.*

THE MOVING HAND

The lady was ashamed of what had happened in the second-class compartment of the express train, and had intended to tell no one about her unpleasant experience. The famous journalist uncovered her guilty secret in a most unexpected manner...

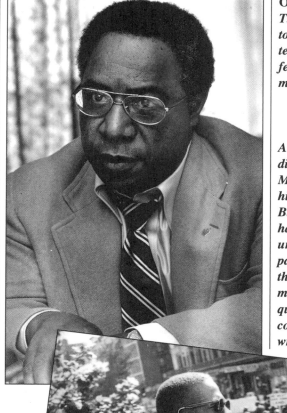

Opposite: *Journalist William T. Stead, who had the ability to communicate telepathically with one of his female acquaintances by means of automatic writing.*

Author Alex Haley (left) *discovered when helping Malcolm X* (below) *to write his autobiography that the Black Muslim leader habitually committed his unconscious thoughts to paper. His conscious, spoken thoughts at the same time might concern something quite different – or even contradict what he was writing.*

The great 19th-century British journalist William T. Stead, the founder of the *Review of Reviews*, was also a spiritualist. Appropriately enough for a professional writer, he was also an adept at automatic writing – which he used as a vehicle for telepathic communication with a certain lady friend. As proof of its efficacy, he recounted the following incident:

'[My friend] was to lunch with me on the Wednesday if she had returned to town. On the Monday afternoon I wished to know about this, so taking up my pen I asked the lady mentally if she had returned home. My hand wrote as follows:

'"I am sorry to say that I have had the most unpleasant experience, which I am almost ashamed to tell you. I left Haslemere at 2.27 pm in a second-class compartment in which there were two women and a man. At Godalming the women got out and I was left alone with the man.

'"He came over and sat by me. I was alarmed and pushed him away. He would not move, however, and tried to kiss me. I was furious and there was a struggle, during which I seized his umbrella and struck him with it repeatedly, but it broke, and I was afraid I would get the worst of it, when the train stopped some distance from Guildford. The man took fright, left me before the train reached the station, jumped out and took to his heels. I was extremely agitated, but I kept the umbrella."'

Stead immediately wrote to his friend to commiserate, and explained how he had come by the information. He also asked her to call on him, and bring the broken umbrella with her. She wrote back, slightly disturbed that she had, apparently unconsciously, communicated the details of this event to him: she had intended not to mention it to anyone. She added that there was one incorrect detail in the account his automatic writing had produced – the umbrella had been her own, not her assailant's.

THE HAND THAT BETRAYS

This is an unusual case of communication by automatic writing, if not indeed a unique one, in that the person generating the message was alive at the time. Communication by automatic writing is usually thought of as the preserve of the dead.

In itself, automatic writing is not paranormal. Alex Haley, who assisted with the autobiography of the Black Muslim and political activist, Malcolm X, noted very early in their collaboration that 'while Malcolm X was talking, he often simul-taneously scribbled with his red-ink ball-point pen on any handy paper...I began leaving two white paper napkins by him every time I served him more coffee [which he drank in enormous quantities], and the ruse worked...'

Haley admitted that the projected autobiography 'got off to a very poor start', but by reading Malcolm X's scribblings (which, Haley said, 'documented how he could be talking about one thing and thinking of something else'), he was able to latch on to Malcolm X's real interests at the time, and steer their discussions so that the Black Muslim leader finally abandoned his reserve. Through these scraps of automatic writing, too, Haley was able to tell Malcolm X's true reactions to current events in his life – which were often quite different from what he would be saying publicly and to Haley. When he was officially silenced by the leader of the Black Muslims, for instance, he wrote: 'I was going downhill until he picked me up, but the more I think of it, we picked each other up.' Before he was assassinated, Malcolm X had set up his own rival mosque and militant black political organization.

The example of Malcolm X demonstrates clearly what Dr Brian Inglis has remarked – that automatic writing is 'the outcome of a different level of consciousness' rather than anything intrinsically paranormal. But that level of consciousness has often proven to be one that is sensitive to paranormal information: whether it is received from other people through extra-sensory perception or whether it 'tunes in' to entities on a quite different level of being – for instance, those who have died.

DEAD CERTAINTIES

In *The Paranormal*, Dr Inglis cites two fascinating examples of automatic writing that seem to have come from dead people and that produced information that no one living could have known by any normal means.

Sir Edward Marshall Hall (1858–1927), reckoned the premier English barrister of his day, was staying with his sister; among the guests was her friend Miss K. Wingfield, who was an adept in automatic

Below: *Sir Edward Marshall Hall, who received news of his brother's death through automatic writing, three weeks before official notification of his loss reached him.*

writing. When she agreed to give a demonstration of her gift, Hall took a letter that he had had from South Africa the previous day, sealed it in a fresh envelope, handed it to Miss Wingfield and asked her where it came from.

The immediate response was: 'The writer of that letter is dead.' After further questions the automatic writing answered the original question: the letter had come from South Africa. What Sir Edward had not told anyone present (not even his sister) was that it had in fact come from his brother, and had been posted three weeks previously. Three weeks after his visit to his sister's house, Sir Edward received another letter from South Africa – telling him that his brother was dead. He had died in his bed the day before the session with Miss Wingfield.

The English healer Matthew Manning found that, when he was a teenager, automatic writing helped divert whatever psychic energy was wreaking havoc in his parents' home through poltergeist attacks. On one occasion the Manning family decided to get in touch with the spirit of Manning's great-grandfather, Hayward Collins, who had been a racehorse owner. They asked if he could give them the winners at a race meeting scheduled for the following day. None of the family had read what horses were running then, and deliberately did not do so until the end of the next day's racing. They found that great-grandfather Collins – or his shade – had correctly 'named six horses, which turned out to be runners: two came in first, one second, and two third, which would have netted a good each-way profit, had money been put on them'.

Collins, later, also gave this message through automatic writing: 'Put your money on Red Rum which will come in first, and on Crisp which will come in second. The third will be a tight spot so leave well alone.' Red Rum won the race. Crisp was second. The third place, a photo-finish, was won by a short nose.

THE GLASTONBURY QUEST

One of the most dramatic indications that automatic writing may genuinely come from entities in the world hereafter resulted in the uncovering of Glastonbury Abbey. In

the process, the career of the archeologist concerned was ruined.

From 1191 onward Glastonbury Abbey flourished, as pilgrims flocked to the site of King Arthur's tomb, which was – so the monks said – discovered that year. The Abbey had a long history: it had been founded early in the 5th century by St Patrick before his mission to Ireland, which began in AD 432. In 1539, however, the powers behind the English Reformation cast their eyes on Glastonbury. King Henry VIII's commissioners executed the abbot, Richard Whyting, confiscated the Abbey's lands and wealth, and wrecked the building. Over the next four centuries its stones sank from sight under the encroaching loam and a tangle of weeds.

In 1907 the Abbey ruins were bought by the Church of England. By then the neglected, overgrown site had become an enigma. The Church appointed 43-year-old archeologist and architect Frederick Bligh Bond to excavate it. Bond was recognized as one of the leading English experts on Gothic architecture and a past master at restoring medieval buildings. Unknown to his new employers, he was also a devotee of psychic studies.

Bond's brief included the task of locating two chapels whose whereabouts

Above: Red Rum, named as a sure-fire winner in a race described through automatic writing by the shade of an English healer's long-dead great-grandfather.

'THE WRITER OF THAT LETTER IS DEAD.'

The presence of the alleged grave of King Arthur at Glastonbury Abbey, Somerset (above), and the legend that Joseph of Arimathea had brought there the Holy Grail, the drinking vessel (right) used at the Last Supper of Jesus of Nazareth with his disciples (below right) made the Abbey a prime site for archeological investigation.

were by that time a complete mystery. They were the Loretto and the Edgar chapels, built by Richard Bere, the last abbot but one at Glastonbury. Bere had also revived and promoted the legend that Joseph of Arimathea, the uncle of Jesus of Nazareth, had visited Glastonbury twice – first with Jesus when he was a child, and later, after the crucifixion, bearing the Holy Grail – the vessel from which the disciples had drunk at the Last Supper.

Bond was faced with a big problem: he

had insufficient funds for a full-scale dig, and breathing down his neck was a rival architect, officially appointed to preserve the ruins Bond found but in reality deeply interested in finding them, and taking credit for the fact, before him. Bond decided to undertake what he politely called a 'psychological experiment' to aid him in a job whose success otherwise depended on guesswork. The experiment was, in fact, a direct appeal to the spirit world through automatic writing.

DISTINCTIVE HANDWRITING

In the afternoon of 7 November 1907, Bond and his friend John Alleyne Bartlett sat down at a plain wooden table in Bond's Bristol office. They were about to make their first attempt to communicate with the dead.

Bartlett had had considerable experience with automatic writing. He held a pencil lightly over a sheet of blank paper, while Bond rested his fingers lightly on Bartlett's other hand. After a false start, the pencil traced an outline that Bond recognized as the plan of Glastonbury Abbey. Then, curiously, it added a rectangle at the eastern end, beyond the high altar. Asked for more detail, the pencil – or whatever entity was behind it – confirmed that this building was the Edgar chapel. It had been built, the writing continued, by Abbot Bere; Abbot Whyting had made additions to it. The pencil also traced another chapel to the north of the main Abbey building.

Asked who was writing, the entity replied: 'Johannes Bryant, monk and lapidator' (i.e. monk and stonemason). Four days later, they learned that he had died in 1533, and had been curator of the chapel during the reign of Henry VII, and that the monks were 'very eager' to communicate. Further sessions of automatic writing with Bartlett over the following months produced a mass of information about the original Abbey buildings. It all came ostensibly from a number of long-dead monks, each of whom had his own distinctive handwriting, faithfully reproduced by Bartlett's pencil.

When Bond finally started work at Glastonbury in May 1909, he was faced with a dilemma: either he could follow the information he had acquired through psychic means, or he could take the view that he and Bartlett had invented it all, and depend on his own luck and guesswork. But in a sense Bond had no choice: the leads provided by the 'dead monks' were as good as any intelligent guess he could make, and they might be just what they appeared to be. He staked his reputation on the monks, and started digging according to their advice.

THE COMPANY OF AVALON

Bond's workmen duly dug trenches at the east end of the visible ruins and discovered

Below: *Monks at Mass, in a 15th-century illustration.*

By the mid-19th century, Glastonbury Abbey (above) was fast disappearing beneath weeds and loam.

OUTSIDE THE WALLS OF THE ABBEY CHURCH A GIANT WAS BURIED; BETWEEN HIS LEGS LAY A HUMAN SKULL.

Right: *The ruins of the Abbey today, neatly exposed – thanks, largely, to messages given to the archeologist Frederick Bligh Bond through automatic writing.*

a huge wall, more than 30 ft long, whose existence no one had suspected. Further digging revealed the whole of what could only have been the remains of the lost Edgar Chapel, precisely where the monks – who were now calling themselves 'the Company of Avalon' and 'the watchers from the other side' – had said it was.

Bond found time and again that the monks' automatic writing was absolutely reliable. For example, they told him that the chapel roof had been painted in gold and crimson, and Bond's workers dug up arch mouldings with the red and gold paint still intact on them. The monks said the chapel windows were stained azure, and Bond found fragments of blue stained glass among the ruins – to his own surprise, since most glass of the period was stained white or gold. Still more unusual was the monks' claim that at the east end of the chapel was a door leading to the street. Most churches simply don't have doors behind the altar, but the Edgar Chapel, it turned out, did indeed. The monks even told Bond the precise dimensions of the chapel, although he was sceptical when he first read them, for they seemed enormous. But they were correct.

The 'Company of Avalon' produced a mass of other information that explained finds at the Abbey; but Bond could not reveal what he was sure were the facts without revealing his sources. One of the more mysterious finds, as far as conventionally available knowledge went, was the skeleton of a 7 ft tall man found buried – without a coffin – just outside the walls of the Abbey church on the south side of the nave. Stranger still, between the giant's legs was another human skull.

According to the Company of Avalon, the skeleton had belonged to a monk named Radulphus. He had come to England in 1087, after the Norman invasion led by William the Conqueror. William had installed a Norman abbot, named Thurstan, at Glastonbury. Radulphus had been Thurstan's treasurer. Before the giant monk died at the extreme old age of 103, he had asked to be buried as near as possible to the church he loved. But what about the extra skull?

A curious tale attached to this, the shades of the monks informed Bond. Abbot Thurstan and his Norman monks were notoriously cruel to the Saxon monks who had had charge of Glastonbury before their arrival, and at one point incited, or engineered, the slaughter of a number of the Saxons by Norman soldiers. A local earl, Eawulf of Edgarley, had led a reprisal attack against the Normans. In the battle he came up against Radulphus – whom he managed to wound severely with his axe – and then Radulphus slew him. He was buried in the Abbey grounds. When, decades later, the brothers were digging Radulphus's grave, they came upon Eawulf's bones. By chance he been buried at the same spot that was chosen for Radulphus. The former enemies had been joined in death, their bones mingling in the same plain grave.

Bond spent months poring over old manuscripts to uncover some surviving documentary evidence of what the 'watchers' had told him through automatic writing. There was no known record of Eawulf; no scholar of the period had heard of him. But at the end of this odyssey through the crumbling chronicles of Saxon and Norman England, Bond had established that there had indeed been an earldom of Edgarley in Somerset in the ninth century at least; the obvious inference – at least it was Bond's – was that this was an ancestor of the Eawulf whose story had been told him by the dead monks of Glastonbury.

A DOOMED MAN

For more than 10 years Bond kept secret the source of his seemingly – and, in fact – uncanny ability to unearth the most surprising new facts about the Glastonbury site. His discretion was not the result of any lack of faith in what he and Bartlett had been told – the times his scepticism had been confounded were too many for that. The problem was the Church of England, which had always been hostile to spiritualism. Bond, already surrounded by jealous colleagues and suffering from a reputation for a dictatorial, even cranky, style of managing the Glastonbury project,

would be bound to suffer if he described his experiments with automatic writing – no matter how fruitful they had proved.

In the end, the strain of remaining silent grew too great, and he decided, fatefully, to go public with the truth. In 1918 he published *The Gate of Remembrance*, which detailed the whole saga of his communications with the 'watchers' through automatic writing since 1908. As soon as it went on sale, Bond was a doomed man as far as his professional life was concerned.

The budget for the Glastonbury dig was slashed. Bond was saddled with an unsympathetic co-director, whose job was, plainly enough, to keep him in line. A monstrous Church bureaucracy suddenly took a singularly obstructive interest in his work at Glastonbury. Toward the end of his direct association with the Abbey he was demoted to cataloguing his finds for a miserly stipend of £10 a month. In 1922 he received a letter that, in the scrupulously

Above: *The restored Galilee – the porch outside the main, west door – at Glastonbury today.*

polite but utterly chilling language of officialdom, summarily fired him from even that lowly position. His career, all too literally, was now in ruins. Even the most scholarly of his books were banned from sale within the Abbey precincts. Bond spent much of the rest of his life in the USA, pursuing psychical research rather than archeology. He died alone, impoverished and embittered, in 1945.

Do Bond's and Barrett's ventures into automatic writing constitute reasonable proof of survival of death? That is certainly what they seem to offer, but one of the many ironies in the way the Establishment treated Bond lies in the sobering fact that he himself came to believe that they did not. Bond himself maintained that he and Barrett had gained access not to the words of the dead but to a storehouse of buried – perhaps racial – memory. This was something akin to psychologist Carl J. Jung's notion of the 'collective unconscious', but one specific to England and the English and their peculiar myths and traditions. The gateway of remembrance was his own intuition, released to run free through the discipline and concentration of preparing for his experiments in automatic writing. The power of intuition, he wrote, 'from the depths of the subconscious mind...has evoked these images'.

Such an argument is appealing, but its attraction may be somewhat specious. Because 'intuition' is familiar to us all, and because so many of Jung's ideas have acquired a kind of veneer of truth because

they have been successful in treating people in psychotherapy, many people feel more comfortable with this form of words as they seem to describe the inexplicable rather than proof of survival of death. In a rigidly secular age, it may even be that most people do not *wish* to survive after the death of their physical bodies: perhaps their worst fears will come true. Perhaps, even, they fear that they could not cope with their deepest yearnings coming true, either. But to argue that 'intuition' is a better explanation than straightforward communication with the dead, for what Bond and Barrett discovered, is merely to substitute one unknown for another.

Sometimes things really are as simple as they seem. The evidence from the 'Glastonbury scripts' for life after death is probably as good as any we will ever have. That is, until we die.

RULING PASSION

Frederick Bligh Bond, curiously enough, was instrumental in a case of apparent communication with the dead that, in contrast, throws up almost every question possible about the nature of psychic communications with the hereafter – ones that do not, however, seem relevant in his own involvement with the former tenants of Glastonbury Abbey.

In 1963, three years after the author's death at the age of 92, an intriguing book titled *A Tudor Story* by an Anglican clergyman, a canon of Peterborough Cathedral named William Packenham-Walsh, was published. It was in essence the record of one man's obsession with a woman who had died 332 years before he was born: in short, Packenham-Walsh's passion for Anne Boleyn, the second wife of King Henry VIII of England, born in 1507 and executed, after Henry had successfully pressed rather dubious charges of high treason, which included claims of adultery with her own brother, who was executed with her, on 15 May 1536.

Packenham-Walsh's interest in Anne Boleyn had first been aroused when, as a missionary in China, he read a biography of the dead queen in 1917. By the time he returned to England, the cause of Anne Boleyn – 'a queen who has been much misunderstood' – had become a ruling

Below: *Henry VIII of England, with his second wife, Anne Boleyn, whom he had executed in 1536. In 1921, an Anglican canon began a long and strange correspondence with Anne Boleyn through automatic writing.*

passion in his life. In August 1921 he instigated the first of many sittings with mediums that supposedly put him indirectly in touch with the dead queen – and with her husband, who was as temperamental in death, it seems, as he ever was in real life.

This first session, with a medium called Mrs Clegg, did not involve automatic writing, but it did produce a wealth of information, unknown to the canon until his own researches confirmed it, about Anne Boleyn. For the disinterested observer it also raised the most fundamental questions about the nature of Mrs Clegg's mediumship. This is not to imply that she was in any way a fraud or a charlatan, but to question whether she herself understood the real nature of her gift (a problem we shall meet again in discussing other mediums and their alleged communications with the dead). There are two reasons for waving this flag of warning.

In the first place, during the sitting, Packenham-Walsh was unable to restrain himself from telling Mrs Clegg the reason for his visit: she soon learned who her visiting 'spirit' was supposed to be, so breaking a cardinal rule of objective psychical research. In the second place (at a later sitting), the purported Anne Boleyn made a curious prediction. The canon, she said, would be 'offered a parish with the snowdrops' and would 'go to it with the daffodils'. Not long after this Packenham-Walsh was offered the living of Sulgrave, Northamptonshire. When he first visited the parish it was covered with snowdrops. When he took up residence there, daffodils were everywhere. The vicarage gardener, according to Packenham-Walsh, said he had never seen anything like it in 40 years' service in his craft.

Even assuming that Packenham-Walsh's account is accurate and uncoloured by his deep desire to prove his particular point, and presuming a great deal of other things as well, there is no particular reason to infer from all this that Mrs Clegg actually was in contact with the shade of Anne Boleyn. She knew of Packenham-Walsh's interest and it seems much more likely that she was picking up information about the dead queen from Packenham-Walsh's own mind, and was dramatizing it as the word of the dead, than that she was in direct

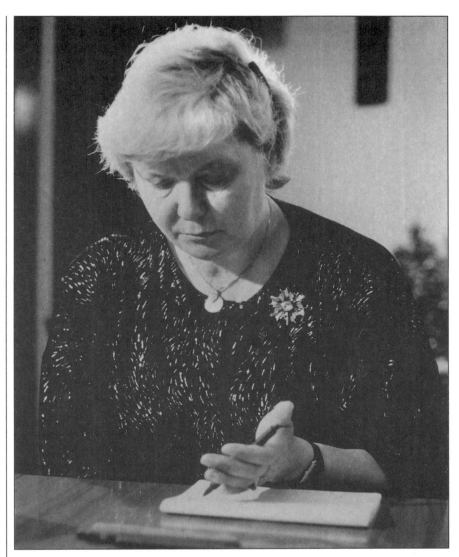

contact with Anne Boleyn herself. This is if anything borne out by the prediction that came true. Mrs Clegg was probably clairvoyant in a wide degree, but her understanding of her gifts had to be translated in terms of her spiritualist beliefs in survival after death. So, she was bound to present – just as Packenham-Walsh, for his own reasons, was bound to accept – her precognition of the canon's future through the secondary medium of Anne Boleyn's allegedly discarnate soul.

SIMPLE DECEPTION

Frederick Bligh Bond became involved in Packenham-Walsh's psychical researches into Anne Boleyn because another medium, a Miss Eleanor Kelly, had received messages through automatic writing mentioning both himself and Bond. In due course, Bond introduced

Above: *A modern Italian medium, Anita, at work. Although normally right-handed, she uses her left hand to receive messages.*

WAS THE MEDIUM GUILTY OF DECEPTION?

Right and below: Samples of writing apparently from the spirit world. That at right is automatic writing from the Italian medium Anita. That below appears to be written in blood, and materialized during a seance with a trance medium in Naples. The writer claims to be Prince Raimondo de Sangro de Sansevero, a 17th-century alchemist and freemason.

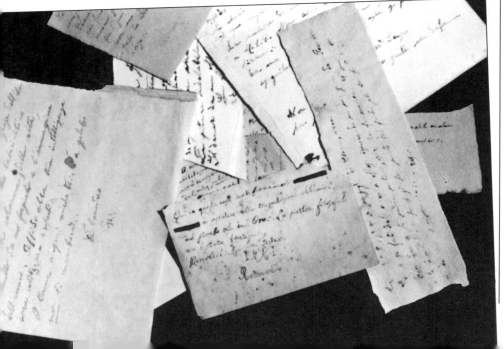

Packenham-Walsh to Miss Kelly, and they began sittings together.

Here, the case takes – temporarily – a more plausible turn. Before meeting Packenham-Walsh, Miss Kelly had received messages through automatic writing concerning Anne Boleyn and Henry VIII, indicating their emotional states in the afterlife. Whether she knew of Packenham-Walsh's interest in Henry's second queen – in other words, whether she was guilty of drawing Packenham-Walsh to her through simple deception – Packenham-Walsh himself does not, of course, say. But the world of psychics is a small one, now as then. News, which cynics would call news of opportunities, travels fast.

On the other hand, if Miss Kelly's interest was genuine and disinterestedly concerned, and if these communications were equally genuine, it remains as likely that clairvoyance was responsible for the initial messages as for the later ones received in sittings with the canon. For nothing in the later messages revealed anything that Packenham-Walsh himself may not have concluded from his by then encyclopedic reading on the subject of the Tudor king and his tragically misused and betrayed second wife.

The basic matter of these sittings boiled down to the apparent fact that Henry was still locked in his ego – 'stuck', as modern psychobabble has it – and was busy either justifying his earthly actions or roundly abusing his 20th-century interlocutors. Anne Boleyn, not surprisingly, approved the canon's record of these proceedings as 'one of the ladders...by which many may climb to true knowledge'. By June 1924 – this time with two other and different mediums – King Henry was wanting it known that he had repented of his misdeeds. Few things can have been more musical to the ears of William Packenham-Walsh, but even by his own account few desires can have been less secret than his to rescue Anne Boleyn's reputation or to know that Henry had admitted how dreadfully he had used her.

Automatic writing, as such, then, is as ambiguous as any other means of communication in establishing the reality of life after death. But the experience of Frederick Bligh Bond remains to tantalize us with its implication that sometimes, somehow, we really can get in touch with those who have died – but who live on elsewhere.

GIFTS FROM THE OTHER SIDE

The investigator had checked for any sign of trickery and was convinced that the spiritualist was concealing nothing. Then, as he watched in astonishment, a fresh carnation materialized and began to fall from the medium's lips...

The late Anita Gregory was a distinguished scholar, a stalwart of the Society for Psychical Research in Britain, and by no means gullible when it came to paranormal matters – she spent considerable energy on showing how weak she believed the evidence was that anything truly strange had happened in the famous Enfield poltergeist case, for example. But at a seance held by medium Paul McElhoney in London in the early 1980s, Mrs Gregory was astonished and baffled when a small, metal model of Cologne cathedral landed in the palm of her hand 'from nowhere'.

McElhoney's spirit control, which called itself Ceros, explained through McElhoney that the model was a gift to Mrs Gregory from her dead father. At the time, this made little sense to her. Only later did she discover that her father and mother had spent their honeymoon in a hotel that looked out onto Cologne cathedral.

Paul McElhoney was a relatively rare phenomenon himself for the late 20th century: a spiritualist medium who produced physical phenomena. His peculiar talent was to produce objects, as Mrs Gregory so plainly put it, apparently 'from nowhere' – otherwise known as apports. His specialty was to bring forth flowers, often from his mouth; however he managed this feat, there was no doubt among the witnesses that they were all fresh. Unlike many other mediums, McElhoney would do this as often in good light as in the more traditional – and for sceptics, more suspicious – circumstances of a darkened seance room.

In November 1981, Michael Cleary reported in *Psychic News* how – though a believing spiritualist – he had carefully searched both Paul McElhoney's person and his seance room for any sign of trickery before 'Ceros' had come through and entranced the medium.

Cleary noted: 'When Ceros brought the first flowers, the lights were on. I looked into Paul's mouth. There was nothing there. Then a flower began to fall from his mouth. Carnations are very significant in my family. I had previously asked my mother in the spirit world to bring that kind of flower. When Ceros apported a carnation for me he said it was a present from a woman in the spirit world.'

SPIRIT GUIDES

It is a paradox of spiritualism that apports of material objects are regarded as proof of an immaterial life after death – immaterial, at least, as we understand the term. Mediums who produce such objects, and who create a wide variety of other physical effects during seances, are called, plainly and unsurprisingly enough, 'physical' mediums.

Below: *One of the most basic effects witnessed at seances in the 19th century and even today – the levitation of a table.*

Victorian seances were essentially middle-class affairs, and provided an acceptable forum for men and women to meet and, to some extent, shed their inhibitions. Mediums might be from any social class; some used their talents as a convenient means to rise in society. Floating furniture (left) *and musical instruments, which sometimes played spontaneously* (below), *were the least those attending expected to witness.*

The hey-day of the physical medium was the 19th century; spiritualism actually had its beginnings in the late 1840s in the most basic of physical-cum-spiritual phenomena – paranormal rappings that gave every sign of being intelligently controlled by someone, or something, that had survived death. Over the next two decades, mediums developed the ability to create an extraordinary repertoire of physical effects with the aid of spirits. (Mediums themselves would say, of course, that the spirits did this, and that they were indeed no more than the media through which these phenomena were produced.)

An outside observer would say that individual physical mediums tended to specialize in particular effects. A sceptic would say that that is because it is easier and better to perfect one kind of conjuring trick than to take on a number and suffer indifferent results. Mediums would reject both those ways of describing what happens, preferring to account for the difference between one and another medium's phenomena as the result of the predilections of their spirit guide, and as a matter outside their own personal control.

No medium claims to get directly in contact with a spirit on the 'other side'. It has become a convention, almost, among mediums, to have a 'guide' or 'control' – itself the spirit of a dead person but one seemingly more advanced than others – with whom they initially make contact, and who in turn mediates between the medium

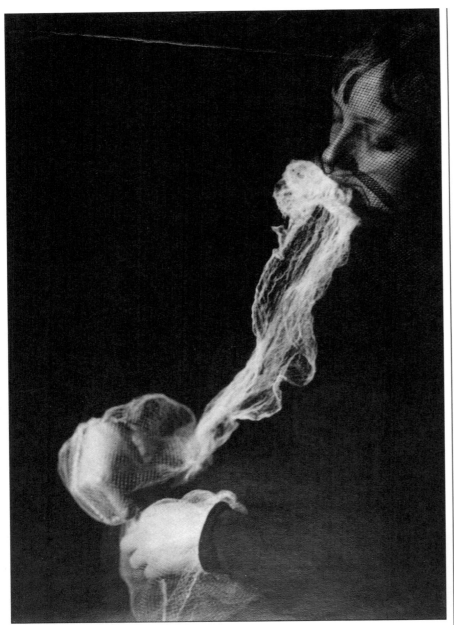

'THE STUFF OF THE UNIVERSE'

Some mediums hear the voices of the dead; some communicate through automatic writing; some receive in the mind's eye photographic visions of pertinent material; and some produce physical phenomena which, they or the spirits believe, offer a concrete proof that spiritual life continues after physical death. The very fact that such phenomena are outside the bounds of normal physical possibility is deemed to be proof that only the spirits could have produced them.

Physical mediums have demonstrated an enormous range of such phenomena to prove their point. Among the effects that staid and reliable witnesses have reported are paranormal and apparently intelligently produced raps, as mentioned before; table tilting; disembodied voices speaking through 'trumpets' (essentially no more than paper or cardboard megaphones), or directly through the mediums themselves (a phenomenon closely related to modern 'channelling'); levitations of any number of objects from pieces of paper through pieces of furniture to the persons of those present at seances, witnesses as well as the mediums themselves; elongation of the medium's body; materializing detached and

Above: *Ectoplasm pours from a medium's mouth. According to one unimpeachable source, its characteristic smell was of body odour.*

Right: *Ectoplasm produced by medium Stanislava P. during an experiment in the 1920s conducted by Baron von Schrenck-Notzing. The baron stitched the medium into a 'fraud-proof' coat to prevent any sleight of hand.*

and the rest of the world of spirit. No one seems to have addressed the question of why this should be so (perhaps everyone has such a 'guardian angel' from the afterlife, but only mediums have the good fortune to be able to communicate with theirs). But mediums find that that is the way things are, and seem to have no difficulty in accepting it. Nor do they seem to balk at the remarkable number of American Indian medicine men or Zulus who seem to figure among spirit guides. That is the way things are. And if one wants to argue about the truth or falsehood of mediums, these are details; there are better and larger grounds for dealing with the truth of their claims.

disembodied limbs; playing musical instruments that were well outside the reach of either medium or witnesses; and, most frequently of all in the 19th century, the production of that mysterious substance ectoplasm, which has been claimed to be the formative 'stuff of the Universe', the prototype of matter before it coalesces into recognizable physical form, from its original, allegedly spiritual state.

There have been reports too about individual mediums who have shown still more extraordinary capacities when under the influence of the spirits: they have been immune to the effects of fire, for example, or have produced materializations of their own spirit controls so real that those who saw them could not tell them apart from living flesh.

Here, we review a selection of the more interesting physical mediums from the great days of the seance room. If their manifestations were genuine then, according to them, so is the existence of an afterlife of some kind.

IMPERFECT HARMONY

Among mediums who produced apports, one of the most remarkable during the 19th century was undoubtedly Madame Elizabeth d'Esperance, actually a lady of English origin, whose more astonishing effects were produced through the spirit of a 15-year-old Arab girl named Yolande, who actually materialized as an entire physical form during Madame d'Esperance's seances.

At a seance held on 28 June 1890, this medium and the materialized Yolande produced a flower – not just any flower, or some sparkling cut hothouse bloom, but the seedling of a golden lily that in front of the astonished sitters grew before their eyes to a height of 7 ft, and in the process seven of the eleven flowers on the plant came into bloom and exuded a powerful scent. If this had been some species of vaudeville act, a professional conjuror would have made sure that the plant was either whisked away from prying eyes and sceptical inspection or equally 'magically' made to vanish. In this case, the spirit form of Yolande was disconcerted when she announced sadly that the giant lily could not remain in the material world, and then found that it refused to de-materialize.

Finally she told the sitters to keep the recalcitrant plant in a darkened room until they next met – a week later, on 5 July. The instructions were obeyed, and at the next seance the oversize lily was put squarely in

IS THE FACT THAT SUCH PHENOMENA ARE OUTSIDE THE BOUNDS OF NORMAL PHYSICAL POSSIBILITY PROOF THAT THE SPIRITS PRODUCED THEM?

THE TINY SEEDLING GREW INTO A GIGANTIC GOLDEN LILY IN FRONT OF THE INCREDULOUS WITNESSES.

Below: *An alleged 'spirit' materializes behind Polish medium Franek Kluski at a seance held in Warsaw on Christmas Day 1919. Crude effects like these may have impressed the gullible, but brought the most scrupulous mediums into disrepute along with the charlatans.*

Above: *Confucius, the 6th-century Chinese sage whose spirit corrected errors made in transcribing his own writings during a seance in New York in the late 1920s.*

HIS CHILDREN WERE ATTACKED, HIS FIELDS AND BARNS WERE SET ALIGHT, AND THE FAMILY WERE FORCED TO FLEE THE DISTRICT.

the centre of the seance room at 9.23 pm. Within seven minutes it had disappeared, but not before two of the flowers had been kept as mementoes of its brief existence and photographs had been taken of the massive plant in company with the medium.

Another reasonable proof, in the eyes of spiritualists, that the dead were able to communicate paranormally with the living was their apparent ability to play musical instruments without the assistance of any visible musician. Such phenomena were recorded from the earliest days of spiritual-. ism. In the early 1850s, for instance, the Ohio farmer Jonathan Koons was, by his own account, instructed by the spirits to build a specially dedicated log cabin alongside his farmhouse in which to demonstrate his powers as the 'greatest medium on Earth', in company with his eight children.

The cabin was not the humble abode from which American country boys traditionally set out to crown their achievements with a spell in the White House. It was constructed like a miniature theatre, and had room for an audience of 30 people. Musical instruments were placed around the tiny auditorium. In this setting Koons and his children would take their places on a small stage. The lights would be put out, and Koons himself would take up his fiddle and play hymn tunes. Gradually, the spirits would take up the other instruments dotted about the room and join in – not, according to reports, always in perfect harmony. At the same time, a tambourine would be seen circling above the heads of the audience, trumpets floated into the air, and ghostly voices were heard speaking.

Koons did not make money from his bizarre presentations, and indeed actually encountered outright and aggressive hostility to his demonstrations from his neighbours. His motives seem to have been genuine and, in the light of the persecution he and his family received – the children were set upon, his fields and barns were attacked by arsonists, until in the end the Koonses left the district to become missionaries for spiritualism – it seems unreasonable to assume that the phenomena were not genuine too.

SPEAKING WITH MANY TONGUES

It's almost a commonplace today to see mediums 'channelling' the voices of the dead – reproducing the accents and idioms of the individuals coming through from the 'other side'. The seance rooms of 19th-century and early 20th-century Europe and America witnessed a similar phenomenon – but with a distinct and remarkable difference. For the 'direct voice' mediums who have emerged from time to time in the history of spiritualism have neither used their own voice-boxes to convey the words of the communicating spirits, nor have they been limited to being the channel for a single voice at a time. The voices, sometimes several at once, have come straight out of thin air to deliver their messages to the living.

New York medium George Valiantine demonstrated just such powers in 1924 in England. In seances held virtually every day over a period of five weeks, Valiantine was the medium for over 100 different voices. Numbers of them spoke simultaneously – and not only in English. The Welsh novelist Caradoc Evans held fluent, idiomatic conversations with his dead father in his native language (not an easy tongue to learn, with its difficult inflexions and unique system of 'mutations', and hardly one a New Yorker could mug up at short notice), while other spirits spoke with equal facility in German, Spanish and Russian.

The clinching demonstration of Valiantine's mediumship came in the late 1920s in New York. At a number of seances some voices that were frankly meaningless to the sitters had come through. On the off-chance that he might be able to identify the language, the orientalist scholar Dr Neville Whymant, though sceptical of claims for the para-normal, agreed to attend a seance. He pricked up his ears and became strangely interested, however, when he heard a voice speak the name K'ung-fu-T'Zu – Confucius – in an impeccable Chinese intonation and accent.

Whymant responded by quoting a passage from the works of the ancient sage. This was more than a matter of finding out whether the shade of the long-dead philosopher would recognize his own work. Whymant was reasonably sure that the passage, though it made good sense, had been altered as it had been copied by generations of scribes.

He had got no further than the first line when 'the words were taken out of my mouth, and the whole passage was recited in Chinese, exactly as it is recorded in the standard works of reference. After a pause of about 15 seconds the passage was... repeated, this time with certain alterations [that] gave it new meaning. "Thus read," said the voice, "does not its meaning become plain?"'

Whymant could hardly fail to be impressed. He reckoned there were perhaps half a dozen scholars in the West besides himself who knew enough Chinese – *and* were sufficiently familiar with the writings of Confucius – to have picked up his quotation with such ease, let alone subtly shifted the reading to give it a different sense. None of these learned men was in the USA at the time of the seance – and

there was no question that any of them would have lent themselves to cheap trickery in the seance room.

A CURIOUS CHEAT

One of the more consistent exponents of physical mediumship in the 19th and early part of the 20th century was Eusapia Palladino. Born to peasant parents near Bari, Italy, in January 1854, Palladino made a name for herself as the focus of the most extraordinary physical manifestations during seances held in Naples. In 1891 the first of a series of tests and controlled observations, held all over Europe, were made of her powers by Cesare Lombroso, professor of psychiatry at the University of Turin.

Lombroso had had nothing but contempt for mediums, but came away from his encounters with Palladino remarking that he was ashamed to have disbelieved reports of what happened in spiritualist seances, adding, 'I am still opposed to the theory. But the facts exist, and I boast of being a slave to facts.'

The facts were indeed astonishing. Unlike the vast majority of mediums at the

Above: *Italian medium Eusapia Palladino. She preferred tight controls over her seances, claiming that otherwise, if sceptics were present, she would be encouraged to cheat.*

THE ACADEMIC SCHOLAR COULD HARDLY FAIL TO BE IMPRESSED.

Right: *Criminologist Cesare Lombroso, whose scepticism toward spiritual phenomena was shattered by Palladino's performances.*

THE MEDIUM CLAIMED THAT IN THE PRESENCE OF SCEPTICS SHE MIGHT EVEN REACT TO THEIR CONSCIOUS OR UNCONSCIOUS SUGGESTIONS — AND CHEAT.

Below: *Palladino levitates a musical instrument during a seance with psychical researcher Baron von Schrenck-Notzing in the 1890s.*

time, Palladino did not insist on working under cover of darkness, and did not hide herself away in a 'cabinet' (a small chamber, rather like an enclosed pew, with a curtain across the front) as so many mediums did – often in order to hide the mechanics of their hoaxes. Palladino always allowed those present to tie her hands and feet if they wished, or take other precautions against her cheating. Another Italian scientist, Dr Ercole Chiaia, reported what he saw at her seances:

'Either bound to a seat, or firmly held by the hands…she attracts to her the articles of furniture which surround her, lifts them up, holds them suspended in the air…and makes them come down again, with undulatory movements, as if they were obeying her will. She increases their height or lessens it according to her pleasure. She raps or taps upon the walls, the ceiling, and the floor, with fine rhythm and cadence…

'This woman rises in the air, no matter what bands tie her down. She seems to lie upon the empty air, as on a couch, contrary to all the laws of gravity; she plays on musical instruments – organs, bells, tambourines – as if they had been touched by her hands or moved by the breath of invisible gnomes…'

The French astronomer Camille

Flammarion reported that in one of her seances Palladino became irritable for some reason. As a result:

'The sofa came forward when she looked at it, then recoiled before her breath; all the instruments were thrown pell-mell upon the table; the tambourine rose almost to the height of the ceiling; the cushions took part in the sport, overturning everything on the table; [one of those present] was thrown from his chair. This item – a heavy dining-room chair of black walnut, with a stuffed seat – rose into the air, came up on the table with a great clatter, then pushed off.'

One of Palladino's most bizarre talents was to extrude, or somehow materialize, human limbs around her. On occasion she would produce entire human forms. In March 1902, one of the many scientists who investigated Palladino, Professor E. Morselli, had tied her carefully and thoroughly to a camp bed before a seance in which no less than six materialized forms appeared and disappeared. As each one vanished, Morselli checked the medium: she was still tied firmly to the bed.

One reason why Palladino was happy to be constrained in this somewhat undignified way was that she was, she freely admitted, incapable of controlling her actions when in trance. She claimed that in the presence of sceptics she would even react to their unconscious or conscious suggestions – and cheat. She was in fact caught cheating on at least two occasions: once during a visit to Cambridge, England, in 1895, and again in New York in 1910. This last occurrence ended her international career as a medium. But it is a curious kind of hoaxer who admits to her own propensity for fraud, and is caught only when a researcher deliberately lets go his guard to see what will happen – as was the case during the Cambridge series of tests administered by the Australian lawyer Richard Hodgson.

ENORMOUS REPERTOIRE

The greatest of the Victorian physical mediums was without doubt Daniel Dunglas Home, who impressed a huge range of witnesses from all walks of life from emperors to elevator attendants, who never took money for his seances, and who was never caught in any deception or hoax.

Home believed himself to be the illegitimate son of a member of the Douglas-Home family – better known as the Earls of Home – and he pronounced his name as they do, to rhyme with 'spume'. He was born in Scotland in 1833, but was brought up by an aunt in Connecticut, in the USA. In 1855 he was told by doctors that his consumptive lung condition would worsen if he remained in America, and in the spring of that year he left for England.

Home had very little money, but he did have a wealth of psychic talent. He began giving seances when he was 17, after a classic spasm of poltergeist raps and bangings in his aunt's home had left him with powers of clairvoyance and healing. Within a very few years Home was to develop an enormous repertoire of bizarre and astonishing physical effects in the seance room.

In August 1852, Home levitated for the first time, at a sitting in the house of a Connecticut silk manufacturer, Ward Cheney. The editor of the *Hartford Times*, Frank L. Burr, described what happened:

'Suddenly, without any expectation on the part of the company, Home was taken up into the air. I had hold of his hand at the

time and I felt his feet – they were lifted a foot from the floor…Again and again he was taken from the floor, and the third time he was carried to the ceiling of the apartment, with which his hands and feet came into gentle contact.'

Then, Home began to materialize disembodied hands. Burr told how one – 'very thin, very pale, and remarkably attenuated' – first took up a pencil and wrote. 'The hand afterwards came and shook hands with each one present. I felt it minutely,' he wrote. 'It was tolerably well and symmetrically made, though not perfect; and it was soft and slightly warm. IT ENDED AT THE WRIST.' Another chronicler of Home's feats described how one of these weird limbs picked up a handbell, rang it, and brought it to him. He tried to grab the hand: 'I had no sooner grasped it momentarily than it melted away, leaving my hand void, with only the bell in it.'

Home gave many demonstrations of such phenomena in London but, lacking an income, had to depend on the hospitality of his friends until 1858, when he married his

Above: *Daniel Dunglas Home, claimed by his supporters to be the greatest 'physical' medium of all time. His repertoire of effects encompassed virtually every kind of paranormal manifestation produced in seances before and since – and some have never been repeated.*

BIZARRE ABILITY

Home's seances were often held in good light, and he never hid inside a cabinet. He produced all the usual phenomena of the seance room: tables tilted or levitated (one, an occasional table with a single leg and claw feet, even managed to 'walk' up onto another table, 'exactly like a child trying to climb up a height'); an accordion that played by itself even when others held it in bemusement, watching the keys worked by invisible fingers; pens that wrote without visible assistance; materializations of human faces as well as his famous disembodied hands; raps and bangs; currents of air; and apports – among many others.

The Russian novelist and poet Count Alexey Tolstoy reported on the plethora of phenomena at a typical Home sitting, in a letter to his wife written in 1859. Besides the ringing bells, the levitations of furniture, the mysterious floating (and dissolving) hands, Tolstoy told how: 'The piano played with no one near it; a bracelet unclasped itself from the arm of Mrs Milner-Gibson, and fell on the table, where it lay surrounded by a luminous appearance. Home was raised from the ground... a cold wind passed round the circle very distinctly, and perfumes were wafted to us.'

But perhaps most striking of all his phenomena was not what Home did with other things, but what he did with his own body.

The levitations of Home, rising above the sitters – 'as if,' as he put it himself, 'I were grasping the unseen power which slowly raises me from the floor' – were part of the standard Victorian medium's fare. One of Home's truly original effects was his quite bizarre ability both to elongate himself and to shrink. He normally stood about 5 ft 7 in tall. At one seance at the home of the art magazine editors Mr and Mrs S.C. Hall, a journalist – a hardbitten species of witness – reported that:

'Mr Home was seen by all of us to increase in height to the extent of some eight or ten inches, and then sank to some six or eight inches below his normal stature. Having returned to his usual height, he took Lord Adare and the Master of Lindsay, and placing one beside each post

Above: *Daniel Dunglas Home levitates himself above the heads of his astonished onlookers.*

first wife Alexandrina, one of the Czar of Russia's god-daughters. With this, material insecurity vanished, and his social standing instantly changed. Home was lionized by the most brilliant and fashionable, as well as many of the weightiest intellectual members, of London society. The witnesses to his extraordinary powers thus included some of the least impressionable men and women of his day.

[Handwritten letter reproduced at top of page]

Two months ago. When do you expect to see him again? In April. He then said without assigning any reason that I must leave Rome in three days. Do you consent? No most decidedly not inasmuch as I have done nothing to infringe the laws of this or any other country. I will consult with the English consul and be advised by him.

D. D. Home,

of the folding door, lay down on the floor, touching the feet of one with his head and the feet of the other with his feet. He was then again elongated, and pushed both Lord Adare and the Master of Lindsay backward along the floor with his head and feet as he was stretched out…'

Hall, measuring the distance between the two startled noblemen, found that a space of more than 7 ft now separated them.

A GREAT WIND RUSHING

Still more extraordinary was Home's relationship with fire. On one particularly memorable occasion he created a kind of parody of the Pentecost. Tongues of flame darted from his head and he spoke in some unknown foreign language while, according to Lord Adare, 'we all distinctly heard…a bird flying round the room, whistling and chirping. There then came the sound of a great wind rushing through the room…'

This was not all. Numerous witnesses testified how Home was able to handle live coals for minutes at a time without feeling any pain. The supremely eminent physicist William Crookes reported one instance:

'Home removed from the grate a red-hot piece [of coal] nearly as big as an orange, and putting it on his right hand, covered it with his left…and blew…until the lump of charcoal was nearly white hot, and then drew my attention to the lambent flame which was flickering over the coal and licking round his fingers.'

Was any of this proof of life after death? Home certainly believed so. He had been a committed spiritualist since 1850, when he saw a vision of his mother dying in Scotland; the mail brought confirmation later that this happened on the day of her death. She continued to appear to Home throughout his life, giving him useful and moral advice. But he believed that his psychic powers were the work of several spirits – the chief among them was called 'Bryan' – over whom he had no control. His work was spirit work. And no one ever caught him cheating.

CONVERSATIONS
WITH THE DEAD

Lord Archibald turned down an invitation to visit his tenant farmer that fateful evening. The blood-curdling events of the night were to make him regret that decision...

One snowy winter's afternoon some time before 1885, Lord Archibald Zealand had been out with his wife, visiting their acquaintances. As their carriage rolled up the drive to Zealand Manor, Lord Archibald saw one of the tenant farmers on his estate coming away from the front door, having found his landlord not at home. Lord Archibald stopped to talk to the farmer for a while and, before he went, the farmer invited him to drop in at his farmhouse later that evening. Lord Archibald had a busy evening ahead of him, and turned the offer down.

Later that night, at about 10 pm, Lord Archibald was in his breakfast room, working. He described what happened next to the editors of *Phantasms of the Living*, published by the Society for Psychical Research in London in 1886:

'I distinctly heard the front gate opened and shut again with a clap, and footsteps advancing at a run up the drive. When opposite the window, the steps changed from sharp and distinct on gravel to dull and less clear on the grass slip below the window, and at the same time I was conscious that someone or something stood close to me outside, only the thin shutter and a sheet of glass dividing us.

'I could hear the quick panting and laboured breathing of the messenger, or whatever it was, as if trying to recover breath before speaking. Had he been attracted by the light through the shutter?

'Suddenly, like a gunshot, inside, outside, and all around, there broke out the most appalling shriek – a prolonged wail... Of my [own] fright and horror I can say nothing – [but they] increased tenfold when I walked into the dining room and found my wife sitting quietly at her work close to the window, and in the same line and distant only ten or twelve feet from the corresponding window in the breakfast room. She had heard nothing.'

Too unnerved by this experience to go

*Opposite: **Doris Fisher Stokes, who for a decade personified spiritualist mediumship for millions around the world. Her unusual talent was to be able to hear the voices of the dead as they passed on their messages to those still 'this side' of the great divide between life and death.***

Below: *Surrounded by his family and a guard of honour, John F. Kennedy goes to his last long home. At least one Irish-American had the promising young president's untimely death announced to him by the unearthly howling of the banshee.*

outside immediately to look for whatever had made this blood-curdling sound, Lord Archibald waited till morning. No fresh snow fell in the night, but there were no signs of any footprints on the ground outside. Later that day, news came to the house that the tenant farmer Lord Archibald had spoken to the afternoon before had killed himself – apparently as the result of an unhappy love affair. He had ended his life by drinking prussic acid – and Lord Archibald's groom, who lived near the farm, had heard the man scream as he took the fatal dose and died.

The groom heard the dying man's cry at about 10 pm – 'as near as I can ascertain,' said Lord Archibald, 'at the exact time when I had been so alarmed at my own home'. The farm and the manor, however, were too distant from each other for him to have been able to hear the actual scream of the suicide. Lord Archibald's wife, after all, had heard nothing.

THE BANSHEE

Occurrences like this are known as cases of clairaudience – involving information that is passed on psychically through sound rather than through visual information. There are many cases of spontaneous, one-off clairaudience that, like the one above, occur only at moments of crisis and most often involve someone's death, but some people persistently and repeatedly hear information that they can only be receiving paranormally. And a few people claim to be able to hear the voices of the dead, speaking to them from the other side.

Among a number of old Irish families there is a tradition of clairaudience that is highly specialized, and not always welcome. This is otherwise known as the visitation of the banshee, which lets out a chilling howl as it announces the imminent death of a family member – though some say it comes to collect the departing soul.

The banshee is not only particular as to whose death it foretells; it is usually heard only by members of the family concerned. Irish tradition says that the banshee may also be seen – either in the form of an old hag or in the shape of a beautiful young woman – but reliable accounts of actually seeing the banshee are so rare as to be non-existent. The term itself comes from the

Irish *bean sidhe* – 'woman of the fairies' – but the notion that the banshee is female seems to have arisen from the sound of its voice.

That, by all accounts, is unmistakably feminine, though the sound of its cries ranges from the most wistful, gentle and seductive entreaties to the most spine-chilling and vengeful shrieks. The difference in the nature of these sounds apparently depends on the attitude of the banshee toward the dying individual and his family. That in turn depends on whose spirit the banshee represents, and how the family treated them in earthly life, for it is reckoned always to be the spirit of a long-dead member of the family concerned.

DEMENTED WOMAN

Tales of the banshee's howl are not confined to the misty Irish past. The banshee howls in the late 20th century as loud and clear as it ever did – and its eerie voice is by no means confined to Ireland. One Irish-American businessman from Boston, Massachusetts, who preferred to hide behind the pseudonym 'James O'Barry', told journalist Frank Smyth of three occasions on which he had heard the unearthly voice. The first time, when he was but a small boy, he was unaware even of the existence of anything called the banshee.

'I was lying in bed one morning when I heard a weird noise, like a demented woman crying,' said O'Barry. 'It was spring…I thought for a moment that a wind had sprung up, but a glance at the barely stirring trees told me that this was not so. I went down to breakfast and there was my father sitting at the kitchen table with tears in his eyes. I had never seen him weep before. My mother told me that they had just heard, by telephone, that my grandfather had died in New York. Although he was an old man he was as fit as a fiddle, and his death was unexpected.'

In 1946, O'Barry heard the banshee the second time, when his father died; he himself was in the Far East, serving with the US Army Air Force. He was woken up at 6 am by 'a low howl': 'The noise got louder, rising and falling like an air raid siren.' On the third occasion, O'Barry was alone in Toronto, Canada, on a combined

THE BANSHEE LETS OUT A SPINE-CHILLING HOWL AS IT ANNOUNCES THE IMMINENT DEATH OF A MEMBER OF THE FAMILY.

business trip and vacation. His account:

'I was in bed, reading the morning papers, when the dreadful noise was suddenly filling my ears. I thought of my wife, my young son, my two brothers and I thought: "Good God, don't let it be one of them." But for some reason I knew it wasn't.'

Indeed it was not. The time was just before noon, on 22 November 1963: the time that US President John F. Kennedy was assassinated in Houston, Texas. The president was a close friend of O'Barry's – and he was of Irish descent.

UNEARTHLY VOICES

As with other paranormal phenomena, there is nothing new about clairaudience. The ancient Greek philosopher Socrates was familiar with the promptings of what he called his 'daemon'. They were, he told his judges at his trial, 'constantly in the habit of opposing me even about trifles, if I were going to make some slip or error'. He had decided to stand trial for his life (albeit on somewhat frail charges) because his voices had not positively advised him to flee from Athens and, as he remarked to the court, he took this as a sign that 'those of us who think death is an evil are in error'.

Socrates, thus, seemed to think that his voices came from somewhere beyond this earthly life. In the Christian era Socrates would probably have been made a saint, and as such would have been in the company of two fascinating Christian women who too heard voices from unearthly realms.

One was Catherine of Siena (the Italian city where she was born in 1347). Catherine not only believed, like other mystics of her time, that among the voices she heard one came directly from God; she seems to have been actually clairvoyant, with the voices giving her information about ordinary human affairs. Some time after she had converted an aristocrat, Francesco Malevolti, to Christianity – and so taken him from a life of singular debauchery – the young man slid back into his former depraved existence. Catherine told him bluntly that she knew from her voices everything he did, and then recited to him a catalogue of his latest doings, sayings and sins.

'When I heard her tell me precisely all that I had done and said,' commented Malevolti, 'confused and shamed, and without an answer, at once and heedfully I fulfilled her command.'

DIVINELY INSPIRED

Possibly the most outstanding clairaudient in history was St Joan of Arc. Born in 1412 into a peasant family and illiterate all her life, Jean la Pucelle, 'the Maid of Orleans', first heard voices when she was only 13 years old. They told her that she could save her country from its enemies – France was then at war with England and the Duchy of Burgundy. Four years later, by sheer force

Above: *The ancient Greek philosopher Socrates, whose profound, still-relevant thought was prompted not by deep meditation, but by inner voices entirely outside of his control.*

of character, she persuaded the Dauphin (crown prince) of France to let her join the French army that was attempting to relieve the siege of Orleans by the English. She effectively took command of the army, and 10 days later the English were defeated.

Other victories followed, and Joan persuaded the Dauphin to be crowned as Charles VII of France. He, however, did not follow up the moral and military advantage Joan had created, and when she attempted to break another siege more or less alone, she was captured by the Burgundians, who sold her to the English. They tried her for witchcraft, and – conviction being a foregone conclusion – she was burned at the stake in Rouen in

The brief but extraordinary life of Joan of Arc, the 'maid of Orleans' (above), was guided almost entirely by voices that dictated her actions and uttered astonishingly accurate predictions – to the extent that the civil authorities gave her unprecedented powers. Her greatest triumph came when she broke the siege of Orleans (opposite below). The coronation of Charles VII of France (right) was another.

1431, still not yet 20 years old.

Such a career would be astonishing enough, but it is all the more extraordinary that it was based on psychic ability. Joan's voices did not limit themselves to inspiring her to battle or to mystical utterances: they provided specific information. They directed her to the one man likely to introduce her to the Dauphin, for instance, and she impressed him less by her patriotic and religious fervour than by her ability to tell him, in a courtier's words, 'matters so secret and hidden that no mortal except himself could know them save by divine revelation'. These 'matters' had been revealed to her by her voices.

There are many other instances of the efficacy of Joan's voices, from her – or their – accurate prediction (recorded a fortnight before the event actually occurred) to the Dauphin that she would be wounded by an arrow at the siege of Orleans, to the information that there was a sword behind the altar in the church of St Catherine at Fierbois. She wrote to the clergy in Fierbois, telling them to look there; and they found a rusty sword.

Joan of Arc made no secret of her clairaudience, and it was this that condemned her in the eyes of the English court that tried her for witchcraft. As a later commentator put it, she died because of her 'resolute insistence on the truth of the very phenomena which were being used to destroy her'. Joan, naturally enough for anyone of her time, believed her voices were divinely inspired. To 20th-century eyes, she was a psychic, but there seems no doubt of her integrity or truthfulness concerning those voices and what they had to say, and little doubt either that they spoke with uncanny accuracy.

PHANTOM STEPS

Clairaudience, as these historical examples have shown, does not limit itself to precognition, telepathy – or to communication with the dead. Clairaudience is really the auditory awareness of *all* kinds of extra-sensory perception, and only a portion of recorded instances of the

Joan of Arc (left), *still in her teens, was martyred as a witch by the English in 1431. To the end she insisted on the reality of the voices that had guided her all her life.*

Above: *Camille Flammarion, French astronomer and sometime president of the British Society for Psychical Research, among whose voluminous writings on psychic matters was an especially poignant case of clairaudience.*

LOUD FOOTSTEPS COULD BE HEARD PACING THE GALLERY, BUT THE DOORS WERE LOCKED AND THE SCIENTIST HAD THE KEY.

phenomenon can be said to offer any evidence at all of life after death.

Socrates seems to have taken his voices as implying that life continued in some form after death, although he did not assume that they came from the realm of the dead itself. St Catherine of Siena and Joan of Arc certainly attributed their voices to spirits, but they were very particular spirits indeed – the Archangel Michael, for instance, was among them. And it was perhaps inevitable that these two women, of such profound and visionary Christian belief, should have identified their clairaudience with the hosts of God. To the medieval Christian there was only one alternative – they were the work of the Devil.

The most commonly reported clair-audient communications with the dead have actually occurred at the point of death.

Karl von Linne (1707–78), the Swedish botanist who established the modern system of classifying living things by Latin names, was not so coldly scientific that he was immune to such events. His house in Uppsala contained a botanical museum, and one night in 1776 he and his wife were woken by loud footsteps pacing about the gallery. No one should have been there at all, since von Linne had locked the doors and, in fact, had the key with him. Then he recognized the footsteps as those of his closest friend, Karl Clerk, but he found neither Clerk nor anyone else in his museum. A few days later, he learned that his friend had died 'at precisely the same hour' as he had heard the phantom steps in his house.

A still surer indication that clairaudience acts as a channel between the living and the dead was recorded by Camille Flammarion in his 1922 book *Death and Its Mystery*.

In response to an appeal for such experiences, Flammarion had been told the story of a French girl named Clementine, who had suffered such a terrible life in the company of her alcoholic father that she decided to escape by entering a nunnery. Clementine's aunt gave her shelter when she first fled her father's house, but the older woman had a presentiment that Clementine did not have long to live. And she told the girl so.

Clementine seems to have had the same intuition, but made light of it. She knew she didn't have long to live, she said, but she would make sure her aunt knew when she died. 'I'll make an outrageous racket for you,' she promised.

Clementine in due course entered a convent, safe at last from the predations of her father. Some time after this, the aunt's entire household was disturbed one night around its usual bedtime by an 'outrageous racket' indeed. There were sounds from the roof as if it were caving in, and the very housebricks seemed to be slamming against one another. At the same time, there was no movement to be seen and no actual damage to the fabric of the house. Clementine's aunt guessed in a flash what had happened.

'Clementine is dead,' she said in a firm voice. At once, the uproar stopped as abruptly as it had begun. The next day, a telegram arrived at the house from the convent, breaking the news of Clementine's death – which had occurred at exactly the time that the clearly paranormal 'racket' had broken out.

UNCANNY VISIONS

By far the most renowned clairaudient of modern times was Doris Fisher Stokes, who for millions of people all over the world came to personify mediumship and contact with the next life. She was a natural star of television chat-shows and stage 'demonstrations' precisely because she was so natural – down to earth, unpretentious, unburdened by any New Age claptrap or desire to surround her talent with occult significance. Talking to the dead through Doris Stokes was an extraordinary experience just because she made it seem so everyday – and at the same time, she seemed hardly able to believe her own success.

In her early life she certainly had no reason to expect it. Doris Fisher Stokes was born the daughter of a blacksmith and a washerwoman, Tom and Jen Sutton, just after the end of World War 1, in Grantham, Lincolnshire.

In World War 2 Doris Stokes joined the Women's Royal Air Force and worked in operations rooms plotting the progress of Allied bombing raids on Europe. She found she had an uncanny and disconcerting foreknowledge of which aircraft would *not* return from their missions. It was only in 1944, after her husband John, a sergeant in the elite Parachute Regiment, failed to return (along with so many others) from the disastrous airborne assault on Arnhem in Holland, that Doris Stokes began to take either her own paranormal talent or evidence of survival after death very seriously.

At that time she had a vision of her father, who had died when Doris was only 13 years old. He told her two things: that John was alive, though a prisoner of war, and that their new-born son would shortly die. Both proved true. After that, she began attending her local spiritualist church. Her sensitivity developed, and she was soon practising as a medium herself.

TALKING TO THE DEAD

Doris Stokes said that she had two means of knowing when a soul from 'the other side' wanted to communicate. Either her spirit control – an entity claiming to be a deceased Tibetan Lama called 'Ramonov' (which is not the form of any known Tibetan name) would tell her 'in her ear',

or she would see a small blue light appear over the head of a sitter, which indicated that someone close to them was trying to 'come through'.

Doris Stokes captivated huge audiences and many individual sitters too. She did so because time and again she produced information from the 'other side' that could have been known only to the individual she was talking to on 'our side' and to her unseen communicators. Yet some odd doubts remain about whether she was in fact able to converse in the easy way she had with the dead.

Doris Stokes has been accused of fraud since her death. She admitted to cheating once or twice during her lifetime. But to

The late Doris Stokes used to attract large audiences, such as that shown above – but she has been accused of fraud.

BUT WAS THE FAMOUS CLAIRVOYANT GUILTY OF SIMPLE, BASIC FRAUD?

Below: *Doris Stokes takes a rest between sessions at a public demonstration in 1984. In the last few years before her death in May 1987 suspicions grew that her shows were not all that they seemed.*

offer some perspective on her mediumship, one has to give personal testimony.

The author of this book saw Doris Stokes in action three times: once at a private sitting in 1981, once at a press conference to launch one of her several books in 1982, and once (while on a flying visit to London) at a stage 'demonstration' in front of a packed house at the London Palladium late in 1985. The first two were highly impressive. The third was not, for reasons that will become clear.

The first occasion was as much a social one (in which I hoped to get some measure of Doris Stokes) as a formal 'sitting' as such. I was not the sitter (an old business colleague was) but over dinner before the sitting began, Doris Stokes made a number of casual observations about my life that were entirely accurate, although she had never met me before and as far as I know heard my name for the first time that evening. Two remarks in particular stand out: 'You've been a soldier, haven't you, love,' she said, 'and you don't know whether to be proud of what you've done or not, do you? But you don't talk about it.' All three of these statements were (and are) true.

Her second memorable remark concerned a ring I was wearing: 'That doesn't belong on that finger! You've moved that, haven't you, love?' The ring was on the little finger of my left hand. It was, in fact, my wedding ring. When my wife and I broke up, I moved it from the ring finger of my left hand to the pinkie, for a mass of tangled emotional reasons.

MIND READER?

The sitting itself was extraordinary for the wealth of detail that Doris Stokes produced about my colleague, some of which plainly embarrassed him because of my presence. But she told him nothing that he did not know already – nothing that he did not, then or later, confirm from his own knowledge. This is interesting because at about the same time the staff of the weekly magazine *The Unexplained* reported that they had invited Doris Stokes to a sitting that – reading between the lines – followed a curiously similar pattern. Settling on a young lady member of the staff whose grandmother had recently died, Doris Stokes found herself in communication with the old lady herself, but almost everything she had to communicate was already known to the girl.

No explicit conclusion was drawn from this significant fact in the magazine's report of the encounter, but in an assessment of the occasion written some years later, the editor of the magazine had this to say:

'When asked...whether she had considered the possibility that she was, in fact, reading the (unconscious) minds of her sitters, Doris Stokes replied that she would refuse to carry on her work if she felt she had been doing any such thing. "That would be an invasion of privacy," she said. "I don't think God would allow that." Nonetheless, the possibility remains that Doris Stokes is...highly telepathic, picking up memories from the mind of someone who knew the dead person [that is, of course, the sitter him- or herself]. These memories are then dramatized by Mrs Stokes's own subconscious, and come to her in the form of voices...

'Presumably the reasons for this are two-fold. In the first place, Doris Stokes has [a] very strong resistance to the notion that she is invading other people's most private space – the mind. And [in the second place]...she has been utterly convinced that we do survive death. She cannot prevent her talent manifesting itself, and so has rationalized it in a way that has brought her, and thousands of people who have sat with her, great comfort.'

SERIOUS QUESTION MARKS

This seems a very fair and logical deduction: Doris Stokes was not – as she undoubtedly, most sincerely, believed – in touch with the dead, but she was in touch with the minds of her sitters. But she was also, it seems, guilty of a quite different kind of touch – simple, basic fraud.

In *The After Death Experience*, published in 1987, author Ian Wilson described how he found out that Doris Stokes packed her public appearances with people (whom she placed in reserved seats at the front of the auditorium) whose personal details were, he and other re- searchers discovered, no secret to her. And the most impressive 'readings' at those appearances were, of course, for the people she had specially invited and with whose particular, intimate details she was already familiar.

Having attended such a demonstration – which followed exactly the pattern Wilson describes in his book – I can only agree with his conclusion: that at this stage in her career Doris Stokes was 'not all she seemed, and the most serious question marks hang over her'. In the same paragraph, Wilson generously suggests that Doris Stokes might 'really have been a genuine medium...rigging her shows through sheer fear of facing a huge audience' lest no 'other-worldly messages' came through. That is possible, but Wilson seems not to have taken one further factor into account.

When he saw Doris Stokes at the London Palladium – and discovered how she seemed so accurate in her readings – on 16 November 1986, Doris Stokes was dying of cancer, and she knew it. She actually 'passed over', as she would have put it, less than six months later, on 8 May 1987. The evidence that she rigged her last big public demonstrations is difficult to refute, but by then Doris Stokes had

become part of show business – whose brave and tragic motto is 'The show must go on'. My own experience of Doris in less clouded and painful days suggests that she did have a genuine talent, and my experience of her later suggests that her last illness at least (there may have been other reasons) combined with a sad and mistaken sense of loyalty to her audience to override her own honesty and integrity.

The real question for students of the paranormal is whether, at the height of her power, Doris Stokes communicated with the dead, or simply made contact with the minds of her sitters. We know her own answer to that question. We do not know the real answer.

Doris Stokes (above) *appearing before the public at one of her very popular demonstrations.*

LIVING ART FROM A DEAD HAND

The teenager took up psychic art in the hope of ridding his family home of the destructive poltergeist, but as his pen and paintbrush re-created the masterpieces of the great artists, he found the demands made on him both baffling and exhausting.

There are two kinds of 'psychic artist'. There are those whose paintings, drawings, writings or musical compositions are guided by long-dead artists. And there is a handful of visual artists who draw or paint portraits of those they see 'in spirit'. What kind of evidence does the work of these two quite different groups of artists offer for life after death?

To some extent the answer to the question depends on the artist involved. In the early 1970s, the British healer Matthew Manning – then still a teenager – began what became a huge collection of paintings, drawings and sketches that were created 'through' him by artists as diverse as Leonardo da Vinci, Claude Monet, Aubrey Beardsley, Beatrix Potter, Paul Klee and Pablo Picasso. Manning did not go into trance to produce the pictures; he simply concentrated on the artist while sitting in front of a sketching block with pen, pencil or paintbrush at the ready.

In his book *The Link*, Manning admitted to being baffled by what was happening when he painted or drew these pictures. He commented: 'How do I ask Albrecht Dürer to draw through me...?...The fact that the person I wish to communicate with does not speak English is apparently no barrier.'

Strangely, what did prove a problem for many of these long-gone artists was how to use colour (Picasso was a notable exception). But this difficulty, paradoxically enough, may be a sign that the communication between Manning and the artists was genuine.

One is reminded of the frustration expressed by psychical researcher Frederic W.H. Myers (through a medium's automatic writing) five years after his death in 1901:

Opposite: *Matthew Manning, now better known as a healer, was apparently guided by artists ranging from Leonardo da Vinci* (below left) *to Claude Monet* (below right) *when he produced his enormous number of artistic works in the 1970s.*

Right: *Aubrey Beardsley, famous for his stylized black-and-white illustrations. One of his drawings for Oscar Wilde's* **Salome** *was reproduced by Matthew Manning.*

'I appear to be standing behind a sheet of frosted glass – which blurs sight and deadens sounds – dictating feebly to a reluctant and somewhat obtuse secretary.' At least the problem shows that Manning, if not in trance, was not in his normal state of consciousness. A reasonably talented painter in his own right, he had won prizes for art while at school, and should not have had any difficulty in using colour if he had been in full conscious control of his materials.

PSYCHIC COLLABORATION

Some of the pictures produced like this were very close to those created by the artists in their lifetimes. Manning – or the Renaissance artist himself – made a remarkably accurate reproduction of a sketch of a hanged man by Leonardo. Another such 'copy' was of Beardsley's famous drawing of Salome. In themselves, of course, these pictures prove nothing at all about survival. Manning speculated on this

point: 'The only explanation I have is that the artist appears to be making a point of identifying himself beyond a shadow of doubt by reproducing something with which he is already known to be associated.'

Beardsley, however, was apparently also prone to make mistakes and to change his mind – as any living artist might – when working through Manning. 'More than any other…Beardsley made many mistakes while drawing,' said Manning, 'but instead of covering them over with paper, which obviously he could not do, he inked over them and changed them into something different.'

These works were often finished very fast – most in an hour or two, and without any preliminary sketching – far quicker and more spontaneously than a working artist would expect to complete a picture. This did not make the process easy, however. Picasso was a particularly demanding taskmaster: 'No other communicator tires me out as much as Picasso does,' wrote Manning. 'After only a few minutes, the time it takes him to do one drawing, I feel worn out and cannot continue for at least 24 hours.'

The Manning collection of psychic art seems authentic enough: but was it really produced by artists in the afterlife, using Manning as a medium? In *The Link* Manning states clearly of his psychic collaboration with Picasso: 'The first work from him came in July 1973, three months after he died. I specifically asked Picasso to produce a drawing for me.' But an equally valid interpretation is that Manning was unconsciously trying out – or trying on – a number of identities through his artistic efforts. He took up 'psychic art' and automatic writing, after all, in the hope of channelling his own inner conflict into less destructive paths than the particularly unruly poltergeist that had plagued him and his family for some years.

Manning in fact later distanced himself as far as he could from the idea that he was in touch with the spirits of the dead. In the early 1980s, he said, 'I have never [*sic*] claimed my drawings to have been communications from the spirits of deceased artists...I feel that I was merely attuning myself to the continuing inspirational force created in the first place by the artist. That is why many of my drawings are only copies, sometimes not very good, of drawings already made by the artist.'

PROLIFIC OUTPUT

Such a statement, complete with its economy with the truth, amounts to a recantation. Such qualms have never had to cross the mind of London medium Coral Polge, but she does not even pretend to be continuing the work of famous dead artists. Her specialty is drawing portraits of quite ordinary people who have died – and she draws them not from photographs, nor from any other kind of image, but from feeling their presence 'in spirit'.

'I know exactly what to draw,' she has said, 'without thinking about it. It's involuntary, like breathing or walking.'

Coral Polge did actually train as an artist, although ironically she was 'hopeless' at portraits as a student in the 1940s; in any case her real interest then was in textile designs. But she was interested in

spiritualism, and became a medium herself in due course. When another medium suggested she had a future as a psychic artist, she responded first by producing portraits of the spirit guides – those in the afterlife who, according to spiritualists, act as individual 'guardian angels' for every one of us – of her sitters.

But many people (including Coral Polge) found these unsatisfactory, since they so

frequently could not be identified easily from the historical records. They were often Red Indians, nuns, monks, Chinese sages or even Zulus, often from distant epochs. They were not the easiest people to track down in their earthly existences. Gradually she moved on to drawing portraits of the dead relatives, friends and loved ones of her sitters.

She cannot produce portraits of the dead on demand, however. 'It creates barriers when people come expecting or wanting me to draw someone in particular,' she has said. 'I draw whoever comes through.'

'I FEEL WORN OUT AND CANNOT CONTINUE.'

Matthew Manning claimed to have had a special connection with Pablo Picasso (**shown above in his villa at Cannes**).

In doing that – without any visual stimulus at all – she has been both prolific and extraordinarily accurate. It has been estimated that between 1950 and 1970 she drew nearly 1800 portraits a year. Three out of the thousands of sittings that Coral Polge has taken over the years will show how precise her psychic vision can be.

AMAZING ACCURACY

One of her sitters was writing a book about the former UN Secretary-General Dag Hammarskjold, who had been killed in a mysterious aircraft crash in 1961. The visitor made no bones about her hope that Coral Polge would produce a portrait of the dead diplomat. Coral Polge did not feel able to oblige – as she says, such a demand 'creates barriers' – and her sitter was disappointed when Coral's pencil began to sketch the outline of what seemed to be a little girl with flowing blonde hair.

Coral's sitter in fact felt doubly disappointed, for she had been told by

Spiritualists often claim that each of us has an individual guardian angel. In this 19th-century painting, **Angel Slumber,** *by Kaulbach* (above), *a sleeping child is tenderly rocked by an angel.*

Right: *Coral Polge with one of her portraits of a dead person, drawn through her awareness of their presence.*

Hammarskjold through another medium that she would have a portrait of him from a psychic artist. At first it seemed that it was not to be this psychic artist – until Coral Polge had all but finished, and her sitter realized that she had drawn not a portrait of Hammarskjold as an adult statesman, but as a child. In Coral Polge's drawing she recognized Hammarskjold as she had seen him in a photograph taken when he was aged only two – complete with long fair locks, not unusual in small children in 1907.

Another had a double confirmation of Coral Polge's abilities as an all-round medium as well as psychic artist at a public meeting at which Coral was producing drawings as they came to her, and then asking the audience if any of them recognized the resulting portraits. Mrs Phyllis Timms, from Salisbury, Wiltshire, was sure that one such picture, showing an elderly man with a drooping, bushy white moustache, was of her late maternal grandfather, Herbert Light. No one else in the auditorium made any move to claim it.

But Mrs Timms wanted some further sign that the picture was indeed intended for her. Coral Polge, picking up some further psychic impression about the man she had drawn, suggested the portrait might be for someone in a green dress. Mrs Timms was wearing blue. Coral Polge insisted that green was the key link between the man in her portrait and someone in the here and now. It was only at this point that Mrs Timms stopped thinking about colours and realized the significance of the word 'green'. Her maiden name, which she had not used for years, was Green. She claimed the picture.

These cases could be 'explained' by suggesting that Coral Polge had picked up her knowledge of her subjects' looks from the sitters – for it was the sitters she depended on to recognize whose likeness she had drawn. But in some cases the connection between sitter and portrait is not as direct or clear as that, and only later has the accuracy of Coral Polge's drawing come to light.

Singers Grace Brooks and Deirdre Dehn met when they were both working on the film of Lionel Bart's *Oliver!*. Deirdre, it turned out, had a talent for automatic writing. Through her scripts, another singer,

Mediumistic art by Heinrich Nüsslein, showing the king of an unknown transgalactic civilization.

'IT CREATES BARRIERS WHEN PEOPLE COME EXPECTING OR WANTING ME TO DRAW SOMEONE IN PARTICULAR.'

who first identified herself as Maria Garcia, communicated with Grace. Later 'Maria' gave her surname as Malibran. Intrigued, Deirdre went to work to find out if this was indeed a historical person, and her research discovered that Maria Malibran had been born Maria Garcia in Paris in 1808. She made her debut as an opera singer in London in 1825, and died tragically at the age of 28 in Manchester, England, as the result of falling from a horse.

Maria Malibran was a real enough person, then. In due course, Deirdre Dehn went home to Australia, and that seemed to be the end of Grace Brooks's contact with Maria. Then she went to a sitting with Coral Polge. Coral drew a portrait of a young

Right: *Maria Malibran, 19th-century opera singer who was in contact with Grace Brooks.*

THE PSYCHICALLY RECEIVED LIKENESS WAS UNCANNY — AND THERE WAS NO QUESTION OF TELEPATHY BEING INVOLVED.

---

woman with a hairstyle that was definitely not in any modern style. All Coral Polge could tell Grace Brooks was that 'This is a Spanish singer named Maria.'

Grace Brooks had no idea what Maria Garcia Malibran looked like, but she did know how to find out. Research in the British Museum turned up an engraving of a contemporary portrait of Maria Malibran. The likeness between this picture from the life, and Coral Polge's psychically received likeness is uncanny. It seems hardly likely that Coral Polge, producing more than 30 portraits a week, would have had time to research this one case in order to make an impression on Grace Brooks. And she certainly could not have been relying on telepathy to give her the image in Grace Brooks's mind.

THE STORY OF DOC TESTER

While Coral Polge gave up drawing portraits of spirit guides, there is a fascinating story concerning one portrait of a spirit guide that deserves to be retold. The picture involved so many different people in its long wait for its rightful home that it speaks for a real and mysterious consistency between psychics, and strongly suggests that there is a truth of some kind in the spiritualist belief in spirit guides – and in the survival of the individual identity after death.

In medium Tom Fox's consulting room in his house in Copthorne, West Sussex, hangs the portrait in oils of a rough-and-ready character who might have ridden the frontier in the days of Wild Bill Hickock and Doc Holliday. The tale of how this picture came to be on Tom Fox's wall is told here in his own words, taken from his autobiography *Medium Rare*:

'In the late Sixties I went for a private reading with a very well-known and respected medium, Billy Elton, the founder of the Spiritualist church in Aylesbury, Buckinghamshire. Among other things he told me that one of my spirit guides was an Australian doctor, whose name, he said, was Dr Tester. Now I'd never heard, seen, or sensed such a person at all, let alone known that I had such a character as a spirit guide. But I made a note of the name in my diary, as I always do put down details of a reading, imagining as I did so that this was some kind of fresh-faced modern colonial type – white coat, blond hair, maybe with glasses, and a cheerful and cheering manner for his rounds of the hospital wards.

'About a year or two later (during which there was no sign of Dr Tester in any shape or form) I was doing trance work in a development circle run by my old and dear friend Hilda Kirby. Among the members was another great friend, Jack Toyer. Just before we started one meeting – I remember he was sitting opposite me in the circle – Jack said, in a somewhat disapproving voice: "Tom…There's a spirit form, of a dirty old Mexican, standing behind you, you know."

'"Oh, is there?" I said. "Well, he's welcome. I don't know who he is, but he's welcome."

'I didn't give this "visitor" any more thought after that, because I soon went into trance. Blue Star, my Zulu guide, came through, and for some time was speaking through me about spiritual development and the world of Spirit. When he had finished Blue Star said, rather sternly, to Jack: "The man in the big black hat would like to talk to you."

'With that, he gave everyone a blessing and left, and I then started to come out of trance. I was nearly "round" when I suddenly went under again, under a very strong influence indeed. The person who'd taken control of me this time said – without any preamble, polite introductions, or anything:

'"Who the bloody hell d'ye think you're calling a dirty old Mexican? I'm no dirty old Mexican, mate. My name's Doc Tester."

'That caused a bit of stir in our polite gathering since nobody had any idea who that was, and I was in no position to tell them. Cutting right across the chatter, the blunt Doc just told them all to stop making so much noise and, in so many words, to shut up. Then he launched into quite a long talk about healing – and very lucid, very informative and, in fact, entertaining he was.

'Doc Tester is a very powerful character, but he's not intolerant: he gently and jovially mocks people, though, if he thinks they're not living up to the best in themselves. So that first appearance was also peppered with wisecracks at people who, he thought, were speaking without thinking, or asking him silly questions. And then, just as

'I'M NO DIRTY OLD MEXICAN, MATE. MY NAME'S DOC TESTER.'

Below: *Tom Fox, through whom Doc Tester gave an informative talk about healing in the late sixties.*

Above: *The painting of Doc Tester that hangs in Tom Fox's consulting room in Copthorne, West Sussex.*

'WE KNOW IT WASN'T SUICIDE. JUST A HIDEOUS ACCIDENT.'

'In the early Seventies, I went to the Spiritualist church at Aylesbury one Sunday – just as an ordinary member of the congregation – and sat down at the back. During the service I became aware of a couple sitting in front of me – for, standing between them, with his arms around them – cuddling them, in fact – was the very strong visible presence of a teenage boy. He was about fifteen, I'd say, slimly built, and quite tall.

'The lady of the couple was, it turned out, an officer of the church, and after the service she made a point of speaking to the new faces, like me, who'd come to the church for the first time that day. I told her about the boy I'd seen with his arms around her and her husband.

'She called her husband over at once, and had me repeat the description. "That's our son," they agreed. "He died experimenting with a plastic bag – pulled it over his head and died of asphyxiation. We know it wasn't suicide. Just a hideous accident."

'We had quite a conversation after that. Their names, I discovered, were Vic and Pam Bradford. The next thing I knew I was being invited to tea with them for the following weekend.

'When I arrived at their house, the first thing I saw on their living-room wall was an oil painting of a man dressed in black, with black hair, and a big black hat. At once I asked the lady of the house who he was.

'"You tell me," she said.

'"His name's Doc Tester, he's Australian, and he worked in the outback," I heard myself saying without thinking. "And that's all I know."

'"Then he's yours," she said. "He's been waiting here three years for you."

'I was completely amazed. How could anyone else know about Doc Tester – especially when even I had doubted that he actually looked like *that*? How had anyone been able to paint this picture, or be sure that I would get to know about it?

'Then Pam told me the story.

'For her and Vic it began a couple of years after Doc – unknown to them, of course – had surprised our development circle. In Northampton there was a medium called Jack Burrell. He was also a psychic artist, who specialized in pictures of the family, friends, and spirit guides of people who came to him for readings. There were

Blue Star had done, he offered everyone a blessing and, with a promise to return another time, departed.

'After the meeting, as usual, we had a cup of tea all round. I needed it: I kept thinking that *that* couldn't be the Dr Tester that Billy Elton had mentioned.

'I said to Jack: "Are you really sure he had black hair?"

'"Absolutely," he said. "And the black hat. He was a scruffy old thing."

'I still couldn't believe it. This wasn't exactly the clean-cut young man that, for some reason, I persisted in thinking "my" Dr Tester had to be. And, as it happened, I personally heard no more from, or about, Doc Tester for a long time – about four or five years, in fact.

two unusual things about his art. He would paint only people who were dead, whom he had never seen in the flesh or in photographs, and he always painted with his eyes closed, because he worked in a state of trance.

'Among the pictures of spirit guides he painted was a portrait in oils of a black-haired man, who was wearing a black hat. Looking rather like a character from a Western, actually, except that in the background of the picture there are sheep, not long-horn steers.

'When Burrell had completed this picture, he gave it to his friends Pam and Vic Bradford.

'"It's not yours," he explained, "and it's not for you. But I want you to keep it. Hang it on your living-room wall. This is an Australian doctor, and he's somebody's healer in Spirit. Someone will be along eventually to collect it. But that's all I can tell you."

'And there I was, looking at that painting, and knowing that this really was Doc Tester. The painting hangs on the wall of my consulting room now, a reminder and an inspiration to me always. I think Doc would be one of my favourite people, with his blunt speech, rambunctious style, and dry style of humour, and I treasure his picture.

'I've found out a bit more about him since – from himself and from others in Spirit. He was an ordinary, country doctor, working out in the Australian outback in the Twenties. He'd spend weeks at a time riding from station to station and settlement to settlement on horseback – which is why his clothes are always so scruffy: they're old, travelling clothes, and they're covered in dust from his journeys in the bush.

'To tell the truth, Doc has done more talking to people in development circles and the like than he has made himself felt by doing healing through me. On the few occasions that I have done healing I've known he's there, but he tends to stay in the background.'

PROOF AT LAST?

The authors of the Reader's Digest volume *Unsolved Mysteries of the Past* comment aptly on this singular example of psychic art: 'The most remarkable part of this story is that three mediums besides Fox himself independently either saw or were aware of Doc Tester, two of them before Fox had [learned] anything about his spirit guide; and the man who painted Tester's picture was someone whom Fox had never met.'

Whether or not they amount to proof of life after death, cases like this, and others – like Coral Polge's portrait of Maria Malibran – certainly confront us with a more than ordinary mystery.

INCREDIBLY HE ALWAYS PAINTED WITH HIS EYES CLOSED.

Below: *Narciso Bressanello, a mediumistic artist who used to be a ship repairer, in his studio on a boat in Venice.*

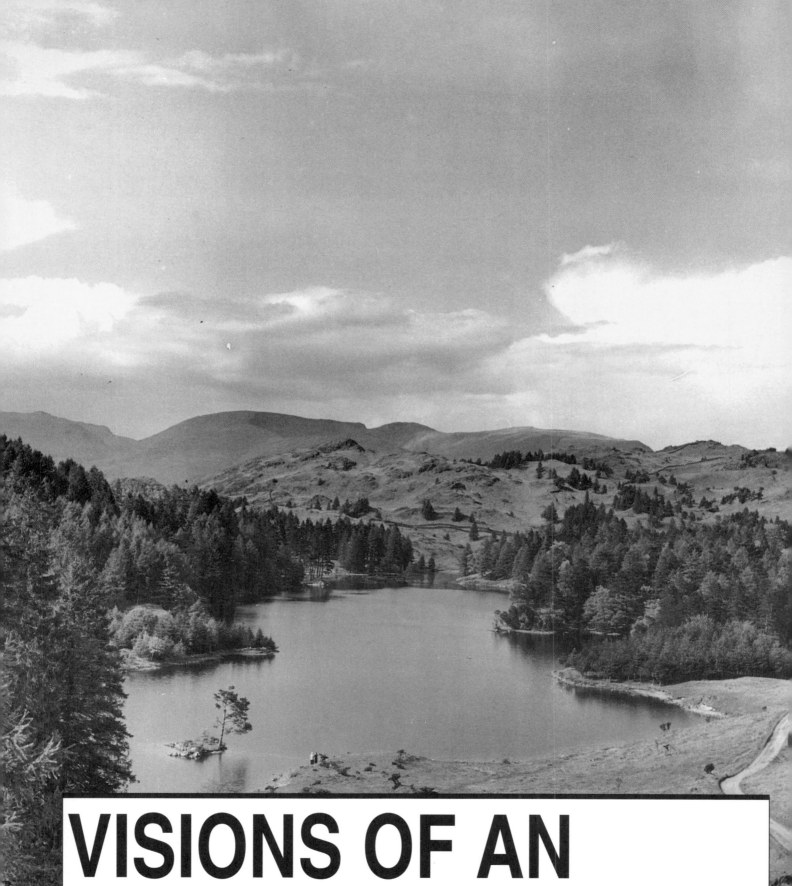

VISIONS OF AN AFTERLIFE

After a routine operation, something went frighteningly wrong. The doctors brought Iris Lemov back to life within minutes – but she was no longer the same woman.

When Mrs Iris Lemov went into hospital for a routine operation neither she nor her doctors expected anything unusual to occur. What actually happened was to change her outlook on life – and death – altogether.

'I was brought back to my room after surgery,' she recalled in a journal article in November 1979, 'and was speaking to my nurse, when a strange separated feeling between my body and my brain occurred.

High above my body I floated wondering why so many doctors were around my bed...'

Mrs Lemov had slipped suddenly and unexpectedly into a coma. But the abrupt dislocation of her consciousness and her body was not to be any ordinary out-of-the-body experience. For while she watched from above, she went deeper into coma and her heart stopped beating. To Mrs Lemov, looking down on the scene, it appeared only that her face had gone terribly pale. And then everything went suddenly dark.

She found herself sucked into a long black tunnel. Light glowed at the end of it. 'I felt frightened and excited as I neared the end of the tunnel,' she said. 'I felt peace, without pain, and free. The light at the end of the tunnel was bright but easy on my eyes.'

When she came out into the light, Iris Lemov found herself in a verdant, peaceful valley, which was 'a sight to behold. There was velvety green grass and calmness. Music coming from nowhere made me feel comfortable and I began to feel as if I belonged. I saw figures of people dressed

Opposite: *This tranquil valley is typical of the visions of peace and calm – interpreted as visions of Heaven – that people have reported seeing when on the point of death, just as they report being greeted by seemingly divine messengers as they slip out of contact with this life, as shown in the engraving below.*

AND THEN EVERYTHING WENT SUDDENLY DARK AS SHE WAS SUCKED INTO A LONG BLACK TUNNEL.

Above: *Kenneth Ring, who has made a study of the experiences reported by people who have, for all practical purposes, died and then returned to life.*

in shrouds coming toward me and [they] called me by name. This man with a white beard told me to go back – your family still needs you – enjoy your life. This beautiful man was my grandfather who died two years before I was born…

'If we could all have the opportunity of seeing my valley during the course of our lifetime, how much more purposeful our lives would be.'

THROUGH THE MISTS

Iris Lemov's experience is typical of many who have clinically died, have been resuscitated and, in the brief period that they have been technically dead, have briefly visited the hereafter. Such people have, it seems, been vouchsafed a glimpse of the life after death. It is not surprising that the experience radically changes the attitude of most of these survivors toward death. For them, it no longer holds any fear, and, like Mrs Lemov's, their present

lives are enriched as a result.

It is only with recent advances in medical technology – both drugs and equipment – that these 'near-death' experiences have been reported with any frequency – for the simple reason that they have allowed so many more people than ever before to be rescued from the very brink of death. But the truly striking thing about the reports of these brief sorties to the next world is their consistency. They may vary in detail, but the pattern of them is astonishingly uniform. Examples of other first-person accounts of such experiences will make this plain:

'I got up and walked into the hall to go get a drink, and it was at that point, as they found out later, that my appendix ruptured. I became very weak, and I fell down.

'I began to feel a sort of drifting, a movement of my real being in and out of my body, and to hear beautiful music. I floated on down the hall and out the door onto the screened-in porch. There, it almost seemed that clouds, a pink mist really, began to gather around me, and then I floated right straight on through the screen, just as though it weren't there, and up into this pure crystal clear light, an illuminating white light…

'It's not any kind of light you can describe on earth. I didn't actually see a person in this light, and yet it has a special identity…It is a light of perfect under-standing and perfect love.

'The thought came to my mind, "Thou lovest me?" This was not exactly in the form of a question, but I guess the connotation of what the light said was, "If you do love me, go back and complete what you began in your life." And all the time, I felt as though I were surrounded by an overwhelming love and compassion.'

A woman who collapsed from a heart attack reported:

'I found myself in a black void, and I knew I had left my physical body behind. I knew I was dying, and I thought, "God, I did the best I knew how at the time I did it. Please help me."

'Immediately, I was moved out of that blackness, through a pale grey, and I just went on, gliding and moving swiftly, and in front of me, in the distance, I could see a grey mist, and I was rushing toward it. It seemed that I just couldn't get to it fast enough…Beyond the mist, I could see people…and I could also see something which one could take to be buildings. The whole thing was permeated with the most gorgeous light – a living, golden yellow glow…

'As I approached more closely, I felt certain I was going through that mist. It was such a wonderful, joyous feeling… Yet, it wasn't my time to go through the mist, because instantly from the other side appeared my uncle Carl, who had died many years earlier.

'He blocked my path, saying, "Go back. Your work on earth has not been completed. Go back now."

'I didn't want to go back, but I had no choice, and immediately I was back in my body. I felt that horrible pain in my chest, and I heard my little boy crying, "God, bring my mummy back to me."'

THERE AND BACK AGAIN

Those who have spent years collecting reports like these – the chief researchers include Drs Raymond Moody, Kenneth Ring, Margot Grey, Michael Rawlings and Michael Sabom – have compiled, from their analyses of hundreds of examples, a typical pattern of events that occur to people who are briefly clinically dead. They call this the 'core experience', on which almost every individual near-death experience is a variation.

This essential sequence of the journey from life to death and back is as follows:

• as people begin to die, they feel a blissful sensation

• as clinical death occurs, they have an out-of-the-body experience, floating above the scene in which their body is lying

• they go into a misty, or more often a dark area, and most see this transformed into a long tunnel with light at the end

• they hurtle with increasing speed down the tunnel

• as they emerge into the light, they are greeted by a relative or by a recognized religious leader such as Jesus of Nazareth

• the scenery at the end of the tunnel is often pastoral – a pleasant rural scene, or a beautiful garden

• soothing or 'heavenly' music is

> **'I DIDN'T WANT TO GO BACK BUT I HAD NO CHOICE…I HEARD MY LITTLE BOY CRYING.'**

Left: *Jesus of Nazareth, depicted as* **The Light of the World** *in the famous painting by William Holman Hunt: Jesus is one of the divine figures who, survivors say, greet the dying as they enter the afterlife.*

Below: *The elect enter Heaven, as imagined by Luca Signorelli in a fresco in Orvieto cathedral. Those who believe they have had a glimpse of the afterlife report hearing strains of sweet music, as featured in Signorelli's painting.*

Below: *The archangel Gabriel, one of the figures who reputedly greet the dead as they enter the afterlife.*

playing, though often its source is invisible

• sometimes, scenes from their earthly life pass before them, as if in a movie. These may also occur earlier in the sequence, before or during the passage through the tunnel

• a disembodied voice from 'the light', or the relative or other figure who greeted them, tells them to 'go back'

• the return from this celestial scene is usually instantaneous. At once, the body feels normal sensations – usually the pain from their injury or from the efforts of those trying to revive them

• as a result of the experience, people no longer fear death. They also tend to express a reduced interest in material things, and a heightened interest in spiritual matters, although conventional religions often lose much of any former attraction they may have had.

A PSYCHOLOGICAL TRICK?

The very consistency of the near-death experience argues for its truth: that there is a place we go when we die, and our loved ones are there to greet us and ease us past the shock of the transition from this life to the next. But that very same consistency can be interpreted in a quite different way.

For example, the highly regarded parapsychologist Dr Susan Blackmore has suggested that one near-death experience is so like another not because we all experience the same actual, objective reality at the point of death, but because our brains are essentially built in the same way – just as we all have noses above our mouths, and eyes to watch over both, and ears one each side of our heads. As our physical system collapses, the shards of consciousness interpret these symptoms of death in the best possible light, calling on the failing memory to create a marvellously benign and reassuring, but essentially fantastic, mental environment. Dr Blackmore concludes that 'what is generally now called the near-death experience is a psychological trick, played by the dying brain on the consciousness in order to lessen the trauma of dying. Essentially, this type of experience is the brain's last fling.'

Indeed it may be. But there are several aspects of near-death experiences as reported that don't fit with this analysis and that suggest there may be an objective reality to these accounts of what happens when we die. The very first problem with the sceptical view of near-death experiences is of its own making. What possible biological reason can there be for the mind (or brain) to have evolved a 'trick' to make dying easier to bear? How did the mind discover that it needed to learn this trick? How could anyone – other than through reincarnation, in which one suspects Dr Blackmore does not believe – inherit it?

Even if there is a materialist explanation for the near-death experience, this strange formula is hardly the best way to express it.

'GREETING FIGURES'

There are further facets of reported near-death experiences that indicate that something real lies behind them.

First, there is the figure who greets the migrating soul, or consciousness, on its arrival in the 'other' world. It would be interesting to know more about what distinguishes those who have been greeted on the 'other side' by standard religious figures such as Jesus, St Peter or the archangel Gabriel, from those who have been met only with a seemingly sentient, all-embracing, 'clear white light', and from those who have had close relations and loved ones there to meet them. While prior

Above: *The City of God – that is, paradise – as conceived by St Augustine. According to those who have apparently been there, the afterlife does not conform to such complex ideas, although it may broadly reflect the religious beliefs of the witness.*

Above: *Gustav Doré's illustration of Dante's vision of Heaven – winged, heavenly choirs floating on clouds to entertain the pious. Actual experiences of the pleasanter side of the afterlife suggest a more prosaic existence, if undoubtedly a pleasant one.*

expectations may create what (or whom) one perceives at this point, the figure (or lack of it) that people see may depend on their earthly circumstances.

It would be peculiar indeed if someone who had had a lifetime of almighty conflicts with relatives were suddenly to be greeted with boundless love and cosmic wisdom by the very same wicked grandad who had beaten them as children. It would be equally startling if an agnostic, who had never been averse to the existence of a Great Creator but had long suspected the prophet of Nazareth to be a con-man, were to find that the figure welcoming him to the paradisaical garden was none other than a smiling Jesus Christ himself – who would then add injury to insult by telling him to go back and finish his business on Earth.

Besides, there is a long and hardy tradition – within close-knit families, at least – of dead relatives coming to 'collect' a dying person and usher them into the next world. And from time to time these bailiffs of the grim reaper have been seen by people quite separate from the person who is dying.

D. Scott Rogo, in *The Return from Silence*, cites a fine instance of such an event from the memoirs of the New York nurse Margaret Moser:

'In the winter of 1948–9 I nursed a very sick old lady, Mrs Rosa B....She was residing at that time at the Savoy Plaza Hotel on Fifth Avenue, and up to the last she was mentally competent.

'Early one afternoon...Mrs B. had been asleep, but suddenly I saw her sit up and wave happily, her face all smiles. I turned my head toward the door, thinking one of her daughters had come in; but much to my surprise it was an elderly lady I had never seen before. She had a striking resemblance to my patient – the same light blue eyes, but a longer nose and a heavier chin. I could see her very clearly for it was bright daylight; the window shades were only slightly lowered. The visitor walked toward my patient, bent down, and...they kissed each other. But then, as I got up and walked toward the bed, she was gone.

'Mrs B. looked very pleased. She took my hand and said, "It is my sister!" Then she slept peacefully again. I saw the same apparition twice later on, but never as clearly and always from another room. But every time she came the patient was obviously elated.'

Ms Moser later had corroborative evidence from her patient's sister's son that the apparition she and Mrs B. had both seen at the same time indeed resembled Mrs B.'s sister in all respects. Scott Rogo commented that 'this story...points to the objective existence of the "greeting figures" commonly seen by people having [near-death experiences]...We obviously need to collect more stories of this calibre...'

D. Scott Rogo, sadly, is himself now dead, but here is a small contribution to this needed literature, which was reported to the author of this book by a member of the family involved. (In the interest of privacy, certain personal details have been changed.)

In 1979 an exiled Iranian princess lay terminally ill from cancer in her house in London, England. Her husband was a doctor with a busy practice, and care of the dying woman fell largely to her elder daughter, Imrana, who was then aged about 14. She was with her mother in her final hours. At some point during that time, when it was obvious that no recovery was possible, the dying princess announced that her own father and an uncle, both long since dead, had arrived in her room.

She actually went so far as to introduce her daughter to the pair, although to Imrana they remained steadfastly invisible. Despite her feebleness, the fading woman then told them to go away, since she wasn't 'ready for them' yet. Apparently they did, for she soon ceased to be troubled by their presence. She next gave her daughter a long lecture on her future duties to the family. This responsibility discharged, she settled herself to wait for her 'guides' to come back to collect her. Her daughter saw her greet them before she finally gave up the ghost.

SWEET MELODIES

There is, then, some evidence that the 'greeting figures' reported by those who have had near-death experiences do have some objective existence. There is also evidence that the celestial music that dying people hear from, or in, the next world is not entirely of their own desperate imagining.

A close friend of a certain Mrs L. recorded the simultaneous experiences of several friends of the lady who, with her son, had gathered at her bedside shortly before she died in 1881. The report was given to Edmund Gurney, a senior member of the Society for Psychical Research in London, on 28 July that year, and it stated:

'Just after dear Mrs L.'s death between 2 and 3 am, I heard a most sweet and singular strain of singing outside the windows; it died away after passing the house. All [but one] in the room heard it, and the medical attendant, who was still with us, went to the window, as I did, and looked out, but there was nobody [outside]. It was a bright and beautiful night.

'It was as if several voices were singing in perfect unison a most sweet melody which died away in the distance. Two persons had gone from the room to fetch something and were coming upstairs at the back of the house and heard the singing... They could not, naturally, have heard any sound from outside the windows in the front of the house from where they were in the back.'

The only person who did not hear this sweet music was Mrs L.'s son, although the family doctor (the 'medical attendant') independently corroborated all the details of the first report, adding that the music consisted of 'a few bars...not unlike that from an aeolian harp – and it filled the air for a few seconds'. In his book quoted earlier, D. Scott Rogo remarked: 'The fact that the patient's son didn't hear the music implies that the sounds weren't from the street, but represented some form of psychic process.' He himself collected a number of reports of similar codas to

Pictorial representation of celestial music (below) *by Fermoni, inside the cupola at Saronna.*

Impression of the Prince of Darkness (above) *from a 15th-century manuscript. An earlier manuscript* (right) *shows Christ at the door of Hell. Interestingly, those who have had near-death experiences tend to see Heaven rather than Hell.*

words 'Go back – your business on Earth is not yet finished' (or phrases to that effect), time after time, in so many different people? This is a surprising and unexpected sub-routine to find in a biological programme supposedly designed to ease one into oblivion.

THE FINAL CURTAIN

It might be argued that near-death experiences must be imaginary because they are simply too good to be true: no doubt most people would like to find themselves in green pastures and pleasant company on the other side of death. But not everyone who has glimpsed beyond that final curtain has had such a comforting vision. Some have seen Hell.

'I found myself in a place surrounded by mist…There was a big pit with vapour coming out and there were arms and hands coming out trying to grab mine…I was terrified that these hands were going to claw hold of me and pull me into the pit,' one such unfortunate told researcher Dr Margot Grey.

Another told Dr Raymond Moody that, as he travelled toward the realm of light during his near-death experience, he passed a place of terrible desolation, full of 'washed out', only partly human forms with an 'absolute, crushed, hopeless demeanour', who 'seemed to be forever

people's lives, although they seemed to be rare in 20th-century experience.

Finally, the view that the near-death experience is imaginary, a 'trick' dictated by biology and designed to obscure the fact of death, falls down over a crucial phase in the core experience. In fact the sceptics do not even address this question. And that is: if the experience is essentially imaginary, how does the imagination manage to put the procedure so neatly into reverse, as it were, when resuscitation is successful, and produce a suitable figure to pronounce the shuffling, moving around, not knowing where they were going, not knowing who to follow, or what to look for'.

Both these kinds of Hell have been reported by more than one witness. As Dr Michael Rawlings puts it, with black humour: 'It may not be safe to die.' Furthermore, the existence of the place of dreadful desolation has had some degree of objective verification.

APPALLING SORROW

In 1961, when serving with the British Army in Germany, medium Tom Fox spent a night at the site of the former Nazi concentration camp, Bergen-Belsen. He dozed off, and then:

'I woke up, and something very like Hell itself flooded my mind.

'No more than five yards away, clearly visible, there was a man standing. He was pale and thin, and a sense of appalling sorrow was welling from him.

'It very soon became obvious that he was by no means alone. His was the only form I could see, but I rapidly became aware of the presence of a whole crowd of souls. Occasionally, at the edge of things, I would see their blurred or fleeting images, as if they were on the brink of becoming

visible…But there was no doubting that they were there. For I could hear them clearly enough. I was being overwhelmed with the turmoil of their suffering and heartbreak.

'At first I tried to close myself off from the agonized clamour of those tormented spirits. They were speaking in their own

Above: *In a more peaceful representation in a French 12th-century manuscript, Christ is shown as supreme judge.*

Left: *The light above the clouds. Some people who have had near-death experiences have felt they have risen above earthly things.*

Above: *A traditional Christian view of the way to the ultimate end of mankind is shown in this representation of the Last Judgement.*

In 1961 Tom Fox was overwhelmed with the anguish of tormented people when staying at the former Nazi concentration camp of Bergen-Belsen **(far right, the incinerator at Belsen).**

'SOME WERE CONSUMED WITH A DESIRE FOR VENGEANCE; OTHERS ASKED ONLY TO BE RELEASED FROM THE NIGHTMARE.'

---

languages, incomprehensible to me, but their anguish was unmistakable…Then, as I calmed down, I was able to distinguish personal voices and individual emotions.

'Some were consumed with the desire for vengeance; others asked only to be released from the nightmare of their experience, or to be freed from Belsen itself, the place to which they had become bound by their suffering. So many people had endured so many dreadful things in that camp, and in so short a time, that to those who had been there, it seemed that only those souls who had shared that terrible experience could possibly comprehend its enormity. Their time in Belsen had become their only reality. And so they had remained, tied to the place, to comfort one another.'

Fox prayed for them, and eventually the tormented host faded away. But, said Fox, 'I had learned more about human pain in those few hours at Belsen than many people do in a lifetime.'

The near-death experience seems to offer the best evidence so far that there is a life beyond death – and that, as might be expected, it is as challenging in its own way as life on Earth.